GUARDED BY LIGHT

UNDERSTANDING DIVINE GUIDANCE IN A CROWDED WORLD

Tina Ketch

GUARDED BY LIGHT
UNDERSTANDING DIVINE GUIDANCE IN A CROWDED WORLD

This book is a work of reflective philosophy and spiritual exploration. The views expressed are those of the author and are not intended as medical, psychological, or legal advice. Readers seeking professional guidance should consult a qualified professional.

Scripture quotations, if used, are from various translations and are used for inspirational purposes.

ISBN: 979-8-9951587-1-4
eISBN: 979-8-9951587-2-1

For information, inquiries, or permissions, contact:

https://TinaKetch.com
TinaKetch@me.com
https://YouTube.com/TinaKetch

ABOUT THE AUTHOR

Tina Ketch is an accomplished author whose work explores personal transformation, spiritual insight, emotional resilience, and the deeper architecture of human existence. With more than sixty published books spanning psychology, spirituality, vibrational healing, and philosophical inquiry, she is known for bringing clarity and grounded depth to life's most profound questions.

Her writing bridges intellect and intuition, offering readers thoughtful exploration without dogma and comfort without cliché. Through her books, Tina invites readers to examine love, loss, purpose, and consciousness with courage and dignity.

She lives in Georgia and continues to write, teach, and explore the mysteries of becoming.

Learn more at www.TinaKetch.com

TABLE OF CONTENTS

INTRODUCTION

Love Is Not Lost — It Is Adjusted

There comes a point in life when you look around and realize that more of the people you love live in memory than in the room.

It happens quietly.

A neighbor passes.

Then her husband the year before.

Your parents are gone.

Friends you once laughed with now exist only in photographs.

And for some of us — the deepest ache of all — children go before us.

At some point, you begin to feel as though the unseen world is becoming more populated than the one you walk through each day.

And a question rises — not from theology, not from doctrine, but from the heart:

Where are they?

Not as a debate.

Not as an argument.

But as longing.

Where is my son?

Where is my mother?

Where is the neighbor who used to wave from across the yard?

Where does love go when the body is no longer here to hold it?

This book was not born from curiosity.

It was born from absence.

It was born from standing in a kitchen that felt too quiet.

From reaching for a phone that will never ring again.

From hearing a voice in memory so clearly it almost feels present.

From realizing that grief is not just sadness — it is adjustment.

Because that is what love does when death enters the story.

It adjusts.

The world tells us loss is final.

Science tells us energy transforms.

Religion tells us souls continue.

Grief tells us something is missing.

But love tells a different story.

Love does not vanish.

It does not dissolve into nothing.

It does not evaporate with the last breath.

It changes form.

The physical presence is gone.

The voice is no longer heard in the same way.

The habits, the footsteps, the familiar routines — they stop.

But the bond does not disappear.

It reorganizes.

And this book is an exploration of that reorganization.

Across all walks of life — religious, spiritual, scientific, questioning — human beings ask the same thing when someone they love dies:

Are they safe?

Are they somewhere?

Do they still exist in some way?

Does the love we shared still have meaning?

We may not all agree on the mechanics of the afterlife.

We may not all share the same language for spirit, soul, heaven, energy, or eternity.

But we all understand love.

And we all understand its weight when it has nowhere obvious to land.

This book will not pretend to give absolute answers about the geography of the unseen world. It will not claim certainty where none can be proven. It will not sensationalize grief or promise signs and wonders to soothe the aching heart.

Instead, it will do something steadier.

It will explore the possibility that love is not lost — only adjusted.

We will look at what different faiths believe about where the departed go.

We will consider what near-death experiences suggest.

We will reflect on what psychology reveals about bonds that continue beyond physical presence.

We will examine the idea that connection may be less about location and more about continuity.

Most importantly, we will ask:

How do we live peacefully knowing that the people who shaped us now exist beyond our sight?

How do we move forward without feeling as though we are leaving them behind?

And how do we honor them without losing ourselves?

If you are reading this because someone you love is no longer here in the way they once were, I want to say this gently:

Your love is not foolish.

Your longing is not weakness.

Your questions are not a lack of faith.

They are human.

And perhaps — just perhaps — what you feel is not the collapse of love, but its transformation.

The world we see is not the only dimension in which relationship exists. Even in life, love is invisible. You cannot hold it in your hands. You cannot measure it with a ruler. Yet it shapes decisions, alters biology, strengthens hearts, and sometimes breaks them open.

If love can do all of that while we are alive, why would we assume it simply disappears?

Something changes at death.

But perhaps what changes is expression — not existence.

In the pages ahead, we will walk this terrain carefully. With dignity. With humility. With courage.

Because beneath every belief system, beneath every philosophy, beneath every ritual and prayer, there is one shared human hope:

That what we loved most has not been erased.

And if love is the most powerful force we have ever known, then maybe — just maybe — it does not end.

Maybe it adjusts.

And maybe learning how to live within that adjustment is what it truly means to be…

Guarded by Light.

PART I – THE QUESTIONS WE WHISPER

CHAPTER ONE

The Growing Population of the Unseen

There is a moment in life that no one prepares you for.

It is not the first funeral.

It is not even the deepest loss.

It is the realization that the unseen world now holds more of your story than the visible one.

When we are young, the living outnumber the dead.

Grandparents may pass, perhaps a distant relative. The world still feels solid, populated, full of presence. The phone rings. Holidays are loud. Chairs at the table are filled.

But as the years move forward, something shifts.

A neighbor passes.

Then her husband the year before.

Your parents are no longer there to call.

Friends begin to disappear from your contact list for reasons that no one can reverse.

And in some lives — the unthinkable — children go before their parents.

It is not just grief that accumulates.

It is population change.

The unseen world begins to feel crowded with people you recognize.

You start to carry entire conversations in memory.

You hear familiar laughter in your mind.

You remember phrases, expressions, advice once spoken.

And sometimes — in very quiet moments — it feels as though the boundary between here and there is thinner than you expected.

This is not imagination running wild.

This is what happens when love has history.

The longer you live, the more love you gather.

The more love you gather, the more you eventually must release physically.

And the question slowly forms:

If so many of the people I love are no longer physically here… where are they now?

Are they together?

Does my son know my parents?

Does my neighbor see her husband again?

Do souls recognize one another?

Or do they move into something entirely different — something we cannot picture because we are still bound to time and space?

Across cultures and centuries, humanity has wrestled with this same shift.

In ancient traditions, ancestors were believed to remain near — not haunting, but watching with protective distance.

In many Christian teachings, loved ones rest in heaven, conscious and aware.

In Eastern philosophies, souls may reincarnate, continuing their journey through new forms.

In scientific thought, energy transforms but does not disappear.

Each framework attempts to answer the same ache.

Where did they go?

But beneath the theology lies something quieter and more personal.

What are they doing?

Are they resting?

Are they learning?

Are they evolving?

Are they simply held in a dimension of peace we cannot yet perceive?

The human mind wants geography.

We want direction.

Upward.

Outward.

Elsewhere.

But what if the unseen is not far away at all?

What if it is not measured in miles but in dimension?

We live in a world layered with things we cannot see.

Radio waves move through this room.

Wi-Fi signals carry voices across continents.

Gravity holds us to the earth without visible threads.

We accept invisible forces in physics without panic.

Yet when we consider invisible continuity in love, we become uncertain.

Perhaps the unseen world is not a place in the sky but a layer of reality our physical senses cannot access.

And perhaps the growing population of the unseen is not a departure from us — but a shift in how relationship operates.

When someone you love dies, something immediate and undeniable changes:

You cannot touch them.

You cannot call them.

You cannot hear them answer.

But something else does not change:

The influence they had on you.

The shape they gave your character.

The way their voice still guides your decisions.

The way their memory still alters your behavior.

In that sense, they are not gone.

They are integrated.

Your father's advice becomes your internal compass.

Your mother's comfort becomes the way you soothe others.

Your child's laughter becomes the tenderness in your heart.

Love moves from external interaction to internal presence.

It adjusts.

And perhaps the growing population of the unseen is not a crowd of wandering spirits.

Perhaps it is a widening circle of influence.

Those who have crossed from physical life may not be standing in grocery store aisles beside us.

But they remain alive in impact, in memory, in imprint, in energy exchanged and forever altered.

We cannot say with scientific certainty what activity occupies them.

We can say with certainty that love does not evaporate at death.

It reorganizes itself into a new form of relationship.

Grief is the pain of learning that new form.

This chapter is not meant to finalize where they are.

It is meant to normalize what you are feeling.

If it seems that the unseen world is becoming more populated than the visible one, it is not because life is shrinking.

It is because your love has expanded across time.

And that expansion changes how you experience reality.

You are not strange for wondering where they are.

You are not weak for imagining their presence.

You are human for noticing the shift.

The growing population of the unseen is not a sign that life is ending.

It is a sign that your story now spans two dimensions.

And learning to live with one foot in memory and one foot in the present…

is the beginning of understanding what it truly means to be guarded by light.

CHAPTER TWO

When the Body Stops, What Continues?

There is a moment at the edge of every life when the body releases its final breath.

The heart stops.

The electrical impulses quiet.

The warmth begins to fade.

Medically, it is clear.

Biologically, it is measurable.

But emotionally, something feels unfinished.

Because when we stand beside a body that has just passed, we do not say, "They are gone" while looking at the body.

We say it while looking beyond it.

We instinctively understand something profound in that moment:

The body is not the person.

It housed the person.

It expressed the person.

It allowed the person to move, speak, embrace, and laugh.

But it was never the entirety of them.

This is where the question becomes deeper.

If the body stops — what, if anything, continues?

Across disciplines, the answers differ, yet they often echo one another in subtle ways.

The Religious View

Many faith traditions teach that the soul survives bodily death.

In Christianity, the soul returns to God.

In Judaism, the spirit enters a realm of peace and reflection.

In Islam, the soul awaits resurrection.

In Eastern traditions, consciousness continues in cycles of rebirth.

Though the language varies, the central idea remains:

The essence of a person is not extinguished by physical death.

The Scientific View

Science approaches the question differently.

It does not define the soul in measurable terms, yet it affirms something powerful:

Energy cannot be destroyed.

It only changes form.

The electrical impulses that animated the brain cease in their current pattern.

The biochemical systems shut down.

But the energy that once operated within the body does not vanish into nothingness. It disperses, reorganizes, transforms.

Science may not confirm personal consciousness beyond death — but it does confirm transformation, not annihilation.

The Psychological View

Psychology reveals another layer.

Attachment bonds do not dissolve when someone dies.

Research shows that the relationship continues internally.

We carry mental representations of the people we love.

Their voice becomes an internal dialogue.

Their approval or guidance remains part of our decision-making structure.

In grief studies, this is called "continuing bonds."

It is not pathology.

It is normal.

The relationship does not end — it shifts location.

It moves from external interaction to internal integration.

Which brings us back to something essential.

When the body stops, the physical exchange stops.

But love, influence, memory, and meaning do not.

And perhaps what we call "the afterlife" is not only about where they go.

It is also about what continues here.

When your son's laughter softens your anger, something continues.

When your mother's resilience strengthens you during hardship, something continues.

When you make a choice because you know your father would have advised it, something continues.

Is that survival in the mystical sense?

Or is it survival in the relational sense?

Perhaps both are possible.

But what we can say with clarity is this:

The body is one layer of identity.

Consciousness, influence, love, and relational imprint are others.

And those layers do not disappear the moment the heart stops beating.

Now let us approach something tender.

Many grieving people ask:

Are they aware of me?

It is a natural question.

If they continue in some form, do they know we are still here?

Do they see our struggles?

Do they rejoice in our growth?

Here, humility is necessary.

We do not possess measurable proof of awareness across dimensions.

But we do know this:

Love creates connection that feels ongoing.

Whether that ongoing sense is spiritual, psychological, or both, it provides comfort not rooted in fantasy — but in attachment.

And attachment is one of the most powerful forces in human biology.

Perhaps what continues is not constant observation.

Perhaps it is resonance.

A tuning.

A relational frequency that does not require physical proximity to remain meaningful.

If two people share deep love in life, why would that energetic exchange simply collapse?

The form changes.

The interaction changes.

But the imprint remains.

When the body stops, something undeniably ends.

Routine ends.

Touch ends.

Conversation ends in its former structure.

But something also undeniably continues.

Influence.

Memory.

Integration.

Love.

And if love can shape personality, alter neural pathways, and transform behavior while we are alive…

Why would we assume it loses all potency at death?

The question of what continues may not require us to choose between religion and science.

It may require us to recognize that transformation is a universal law.

Caterpillars become butterflies.

Water becomes vapor.

Matter becomes energy.

Perhaps death is not a vanishing — but a transition of expression.

Not loss of existence — but adjustment of presence.

And if that is so, then our grief is not proof that love has ended.

It is proof that love must now be experienced differently.

The body stops.

But the story does not evaporate.

It changes chapters.

And learning how to read that next chapter — without fear, without fantasy, without denial — is part of what this journey is about.

Because if love continues in any form, then we are not abandoned.

We are adjusted.

And adjustment, though painful, is not extinction.

It is transformation.

CHAPTER THREE

Where Are They? The Human Need for Location

After the funeral.

After the casseroles.

After the sympathy cards have been opened and set aside…

The question becomes quieter, but sharper:

Where are they right now?

Not philosophically.

Not poetically.

Right now.

Are they somewhere specific?

Are they together?

Are they conscious?

Are they waiting?

The human mind struggles with abstraction.

We want coordinates.

We want direction.

Up there.

Out there.

Somewhere.

When children ask where someone has gone, adults often point upward. Heaven becomes sky. The sky becomes distance. Distance becomes separation.

But what if “where” is the wrong category?

Our brains are wired for physical space.

We live in length, width, height.

We move through time minute by minute.

But modern physics has already shown us that reality is layered far beyond what our senses perceive.

There are frequencies we cannot hear.

Light spectrums we cannot see.

Dimensions mathematically possible but experientially inaccessible.

We do not panic about these unseen layers.

We accept that they exist beyond our perception.

So when we ask, “Where are they?” we may be asking a three-dimensional question about a multi-dimensional possibility.

Perhaps they are not “up.”

Perhaps they are not “far.”

Perhaps they are not even somewhere in the way we understand space.

Perhaps they exist in a different mode of being.

This is where humility must guide us.

No living person can provide a verified map of the afterlife.

Anyone who claims detailed geography steps beyond what can be proven.

But across cultures, near-death experiences share common themes:

A sense of peace.

Release from pain.

A feeling of expansion.

Encounters with light.

Reunion imagery.

These accounts are not uniform, yet they often carry similar emotional tones: clarity, love, and absence of fear.

That alone tells us something important.

If consciousness continues in any form, it may not resemble our current structure of time and space.

Think of a dream.

While dreaming, you experience full environments.

You feel present.

You interact.

Yet your physical body remains still in bed.

Consciousness is already capable of operating in layers.

So when we ask where our loved ones are, perhaps the deeper question is:

In what state are they?

Are they in torment?

Are they in confusion?

Are they in peace?

Grieving hearts often fear suffering.

We imagine loneliness.

We imagine disorientation.

But most religious and spiritual traditions — even those that differ widely — agree on one thing:

Death brings release from physical pain.

That alone offers comfort.

The body, with its illness, aging, and limitation, no longer restricts them.

The breath that once struggled no longer labors.

The heart that once faltered no longer strains.

In that sense, something improves.

But what about connection?

Are they alone?

Here we must return to love.

If love binds us so strongly in life, why would that bond fragment in death?

Whether in heaven, in rest, in another plane of consciousness, or in a transformed energetic state — it is difficult to imagine love dissolving into isolation.

The love you felt was real.

Real things do not simply disintegrate without trace.

They transform.

You may not know their coordinates.

But you can trust that love does not move into chaos.

It moves into order.

And perhaps the unseen realm is not a crowded waiting room of wandering spirits.

Perhaps it is structured.

Harmonized.

Guided by laws we do not yet understand.

We assume confusion because we fear it.

But what if clarity replaces confusion at death?

What if understanding expands rather than contracts?

When we release our need for physical mapping, a gentler idea emerges:

They are not lost in space.

They are shifted in state.

And maybe the better question is not "Where are they?"

But "How does love connect us now?"

Because even without visible proof, you still feel them.

Not in a constant mystical way.

But in subtle shifts:

A memory that surfaces exactly when needed.

A calmness that arrives during distress.

A sense of internal companionship during loneliness.

Is that spiritual presence?

Is it neurological integration?

It may not require us to choose.

It may simply reflect that relationship does not rely solely on proximity.

The human need for location is understandable.

But love has never required coordinates.

You have loved people across continents.

You have felt close to someone who was physically distant.

Distance has never been the final word in connection.

So perhaps death is not ultimate distance.

Perhaps it is ultimate transformation of proximity.

You cannot reach them the same way.

But you are not disconnected from the influence they carry.

And that may be the beginning of peace.

We may not know exactly where they are.

But we can trust this:

They are not nowhere.

And love does not relocate into emptiness.

It adjusts into a form we are still learning to understand.

And in that adjustment, something sacred remains intact.

CHAPTER FOUR

Are They With Us? Presence, Memory, and the Space Between

After we ask, *Where are they?*

The next question comes almost immediately:

Are they with us?

Not somewhere abstract.

Not in theory.

But here.

When the house is quiet.

When you sit alone.

When you walk past their photograph.

When you feel something you cannot quite explain.

Are they near?

This is where many people hesitate to speak openly.

Because the moment we say, "Sometimes I feel them," we worry we will sound foolish, unstable, or overly mystical.

But let us slow this down.

What does it mean to "feel" someone?

When your child was away at school, you still felt them in your heart.

When your spouse traveled, you still sensed their presence in the home.

Presence has never required physical proximity to be experienced.

So what are we feeling after death?

There are three possibilities — and they are not mutually exclusive.

1. Memory as Living Energy

The human brain is not a filing cabinet.

It does not store memories as static photographs.

It stores them as living neural pathways — patterns that activate emotion, sensation, even bodily response.

When you remember your son's laugh, your body can react as though you are hearing it.

When you recall your mother's embrace, your nervous system can soften.

Memory is not passive.

It is active.

So sometimes what we interpret as "presence" may be the deep activation of bonded neural networks — the continuing bond psychology describes.

That does not make it lesser.

It makes it powerful.

Love has altered your brain structure.

That alteration remains.

2. Emotional Resonance

We are relational beings.

When someone shapes us profoundly, their influence becomes part of our internal compass.

You may pause before making a decision and think, *What would he say?*

You may respond to hardship with strength because she taught you how.

In that sense, they are with you.

Not as hovering spirits — but as integrated wisdom.

Their voice has become part of your voice.

That is not fantasy.

That is development.

3. Spiritual Continuity

And then there is the possibility that many traditions affirm:

That consciousness continues in a form we cannot see.

If this is true, presence may not mean constant observation or interference.

It may mean awareness exists without physical interaction.

Here we must tread carefully.

Healthy spirituality does not assume the departed are monitoring every movement, controlling events, or manipulating circumstances.

That path leads to fear or dependency.

But it is also unnecessary to dismiss every sense of comfort as mere imagination.

Perhaps there are moments when the veil feels thin.

Perhaps love operates across dimensions in ways we do not fully understand.

The key is balance.

Presence should bring peace — not anxiety.

It should feel steady — not dramatic.

It should ground you — not pull you away from reality.

If a sensed presence causes fear, obsession, or detachment from life, it requires grounding and discernment.

But if it brings calm reassurance, warmth, or courage to move forward, it may simply reflect that love has not vanished.

Now let us address something tender.

Many grieving hearts long for signs.

A feather.

A song on the radio.

A dream.

A sudden flicker of light.

Are these messages?

They may be.

Or they may be meaning-making.

The human mind is designed to connect patterns.

When you see something that reminds you of someone you love, your brain lights up with association.

That does not diminish the comfort.

In fact, it shows how deeply intertwined love and perception are.

The danger lies only in building dependency on constant external confirmation.

Love does not require constant proof to remain real.

It remains because it shaped you.

Perhaps the safest way to hold this question is this:

Whether through memory, influence, or spiritual continuity, your loved one's impact is still active in your life.

They are not walking beside you in the grocery store in visible form.

But neither are they erased from existence.

They exist now in a space between physical absence and emotional presence.

And that space is sacred.

You do not have to define it precisely.

You only have to live within it with steadiness.

You are allowed to feel comfort without claiming certainty.

You are allowed to sense connection without losing grounding.

You are allowed to miss them without believing they are lost.

Because love does not require physical nearness to remain influential.

It requires only that it once existed.

And if it once existed deeply, it does not disappear quietly.

It becomes part of you.

And perhaps that is one of the ways we are guarded by light —

Not because spirits surround us in dramatic display,

But because the love that shaped us continues to guide us gently forward.

CHAPTER FIVE

What the World Believes: Heaven, Return, and Rest

When someone we love dies, our personal grief meets a much older conversation.

Long before we were born, long before our own losses reshaped us, humanity has been asking the same question:

What happens next?

Across continents and centuries, cultures have formed answers — not only to explain death, but to steady the living.

This chapter is not about proving one belief over another.

It is about recognizing something deeply comforting:

No civilization has ever believed that love simply collapses into nothing.

Heaven: The Promise of Reunion

In Christianity, heaven is described as a place of peace, restoration, and reunion.

Tears are wiped away.

Pain is removed.

Souls are held in the presence of God.

The image is relational.

It suggests recognition.

It suggests continuity.

The comfort of heaven is not only safety — it is belonging.

For many grieving hearts, this belief provides an anchor:

They are not alone.

They are not wandering.

They are received.

Whether one interprets heaven literally, symbolically, or spiritually, the core message remains powerful:

Love is preserved.

Paradise and Waiting

In Islamic teaching, the soul enters a state of awareness after death, awaiting final resurrection. There is accountability, but there is also mercy.

In Jewish tradition, the afterlife is described more subtly — often as a world to come, a place of closeness to God, or a resting of the soul.

These traditions emphasize something essential:

Death is not disappearance.

It is transition.

The soul is not erased.

It moves into another state of existence.

Reincarnation: The Journey Continues

In Hindu and Buddhist traditions, life is cyclical.

The soul — or consciousness — continues through many lifetimes, learning and evolving.

Death becomes not an ending, but a doorway.

The form changes.

The identity may change.

But the essence continues its development.

For some, this view offers comfort in growth — that no experience is wasted, and no love is meaningless.

If souls return, then separation may not be permanent.

Ancestral Continuity

Many Indigenous traditions hold that ancestors remain connected to the living — not as intrusive spirits, but as part of the spiritual fabric of community.

They are honored.

Remembered.

Consulted in ritual.

Integrated into daily life.

In these traditions, death shifts status — not relevance.

The departed become part of the collective strength of the living.

A Common Thread

Though the language differs — heaven, paradise, reincarnation, ancestral realm — there is a striking consistency:

Human beings resist the idea that love ends in emptiness.

We intuit continuation.

We imagine structure.

We hope for recognition.

Why?

Perhaps because love feels too significant to dissolve.

It shapes our character.

It alters our biology.

It changes our decisions.

It leaves permanent imprint.

Something that powerful does not feel disposable.

Even those who hold a strictly scientific worldview often describe their loved ones as "living on" through legacy, influence, and memory.

Different vocabulary.

Same instinct.

Continuation.

Why So Many Stories?

If beliefs vary, does that mean none are true?

Or does it mean that human understanding is limited by perspective?

When people describe the same mountain from different sides, the descriptions vary — yet the mountain remains.

Perhaps our concepts of the afterlife reflect cultural lenses attempting to describe something beyond full comprehension.

No one has returned with measurable data.

But countless people across history have sensed that existence does not simply terminate.

And grief itself suggests something more.

If death were merely biological shutdown, why does love resist so fiercely?

Why does longing feel so persistent?

Why does the bond refuse to vanish, even when logic insists the body is gone?

A Gentle Integration

This book does not require you to adopt one doctrine.

It invites you to recognize something broader:

Across religion, spirituality, and philosophy, humanity agrees on one thing — Love is not meaningless.

And if love is not meaningless, then death cannot be mere erasure.

Perhaps the specifics remain mysterious.

But mystery is not the same as absence.

The world's beliefs do not solve the ache of loss.

But they do offer reassurance that you are not alone in your questioning.

Every culture.

Every century.

Every grieving heart.

We have all stood at this threshold.

And across all differences, one quiet conviction echoes:

Something continues.

Whether that continuation is called heaven, return, rest, or transformation…

It suggests that your love is not foolish.

It suggests that what you shared was not temporary noise in the universe.

It suggests that death changes form — but does not nullify meaning.

And perhaps that is where comfort begins.

Not in certainty.

But in the shared human refusal to believe that love simply disappears.

CHAPTER SIX

The Science of Continuity: Energy, Memory, and the Unseen

If religion offers language for hope, science offers language for structure.

And while science does not define heaven, it does define transformation.

One of the most foundational laws in physics states:

Energy cannot be created or destroyed.

It can only change form.

This is not poetry.

It is principle.

The human body is an intricate electrical system.

Neurons fire in patterns.

The heart pulses through bioelectrical rhythm.

Cells communicate through measurable signals.

At death, those patterns cease in their current organization.

But cessation of pattern is not annihilation of energy.

It is reorganization.

The heat disperses.

The electrical impulses stop firing in structured rhythm.

The chemistry alters.

Transformation occurs.

Science cannot confirm that personal consciousness continues as an individual identity. It does not measure souls.

But it confirms something powerful:

Nothing simply vanishes.

Matter rearranges.

Energy disperses.

Systems change state.

Even the stars collapse into new forms.

So when we ask, "Are they gone?" science quietly answers:

Gone from this configuration.

Not erased from existence.

Now let us move from physics to biology.

Attachment research shows that when we bond deeply with another human being, our nervous systems synchronize.

Heart rhythms align.

Stress levels adjust in one another's presence.

Neural pathways develop in response to relational experience.

Love is not abstract.

It physically rewires the brain.

When someone we love dies, those neural pathways do not disappear overnight.

They remain active.

This is why we still "hear" their voice in our thoughts.

This is why certain memories trigger immediate emotion.

This is why grief feels physical.

The relationship was embodied.

And the embodiment leaves imprint.

Psychologists call this “continuing bonds.”

It was once believed that healthy grief required detachment.

Modern research now suggests the opposite.

Healthy grief often involves integration.

The relationship shifts from external interaction to internal presence.

That shift is not delusion.

It is adaptation.

You are not clinging when you remember.

You are reorganizing attachment.

Now consider something subtle.

When we love someone, we exchange more than words.

We exchange energy.

We influence posture, tone, belief, worldview.

Their patterns affect ours.

Your child’s laughter changed your chemistry.

Your parent’s discipline shaped your resilience.

Your spouse’s comfort regulated your stress.

These exchanges do not evaporate at death.

They remain in the system they helped build — you.

In that sense, love continues biologically.

Not mystically.

But measurably.

Now let us move to something more mysterious — consciousness itself.

Neuroscience continues to explore what consciousness actually is.

Is it purely brain-generated?

Is it emergent from complex systems?

Is it fundamental to reality itself?

Even among scientists, consensus is not complete.

Some physicists propose that consciousness may be more deeply woven into the fabric of reality than previously understood.

This does not prove personal survival after death.

But it leaves the question open.

And openness is not weakness.

It is intellectual honesty.

Science does not say, "Nothing continues."

It says, "We do not yet fully understand what consciousness is."

That distinction matters.

Because if consciousness is not fully explained, then its cessation cannot be fully explained either.

Now let us bring this back to something grounded.

Whether consciousness survives as identity, whether it transforms into something larger, or whether it becomes integrated into a broader field of reality —

One truth remains steady:

The love shared between two people alters both permanently.

That alteration does not reverse when one dies.

It persists.

Not as ghostly interference.

Not as superstition.

But as structural change.

When the body stops, transformation begins.

When the voice quiets, influence remains.

When the physical exchange ends, internal integration continues.

Science may not map heaven.

But it confirms continuity.

Energy shifts.

Systems reorganize.

Nothing collapses into nothing.

And perhaps this offers a steady kind of comfort.

Not dramatic.

Not sentimental.

But stable.

You do not need mystical proof to believe your love still matters.

It matters because it shaped reality.

It shaped your nervous system.

It shaped your decisions.

It shaped who you became.

That is not erased by death.

It is adjusted.

And if something as measurable as neural wiring can preserve relational imprint…

Then perhaps love is not fragile at all.

Perhaps it is one of the most enduring forces we know.

Not lost.

Reorganized.

Not destroyed.

Transformed.

And transformation is not the enemy of love.

It is one of its oldest companions.

PART II – THE EXPANSION OF UNDERSTANDING

CHAPTER SEVEN

Grief Is Not Doubt — It Is Adjustment

There is something important we must say clearly:

Grief is not a lack of faith.

It is not weakness.

It is not confusion.

It is not spiritual failure.

It is adjustment.

When someone dies, your entire relational structure changes.

You do not simply lose a person.

You lose a pattern.

You lose:

The way your phone would light up with their name.

The sound of their footsteps in the hall.

The familiar tone in everyday conversation.

The small, ordinary exchanges that anchored your days.

Grief is the nervous system learning a new pattern.

And that learning takes time.

We often assume that if we believe love continues, we should not hurt so deeply.

But that is not how attachment works.

You can believe in heaven and still ache.

You can believe in reincarnation and still feel empty.

You can believe in energy transformation and still cry at night.

Because belief does not replace physical absence.

The body misses the body.

Your nervous system misses regulation.

Your habits miss reinforcement.

Your daily rhythms miss synchronization.

Grief is not doubt.

It is the recalibration of attachment.

When someone is physically present, your brain predicts their availability.

You expect them to answer.

You expect them to appear.

You expect their presence in certain spaces.

When that prediction is broken, the system protests.

That protest feels like pain.

Not because love ended.

But because pattern changed.

There is something deeply human about this.

If love did not hurt when altered, it would not have mattered while it was here.

The depth of grief reflects the depth of bond.

Now let us move gently into something many people hesitate to admit.

Sometimes grief feels confusing.

You may feel peace one moment — certain that your loved one is safe.

Then suddenly, without warning, you feel raw.

Tears surface.

Anger rises.

Questions return.

This does not mean you are moving backward.

It means adjustment is not linear.

The brain updates gradually.

Attachment reorganizes in layers.

You may understand intellectually that love continues.

But your body still reaches for what it can no longer touch.

And that is not failure.

It is biology.

Over time, something shifts.

The sharp edge of grief softens.

The constant ache becomes quieter.

Not because you have forgotten.

But because integration is occurring.

Their voice becomes guidance instead of absence.

Their memory becomes warmth instead of shock.

Their influence becomes strength instead of pain.

This is not "getting over" someone.

It is carrying them differently.

At first, grief feels like weight.

Later, it begins to feel like depth.

You realize something subtle:

They are not gone from your life story.

They are woven into it.

You speak differently because of them.

You love differently because of them.

You move through hardship differently because of them.

Grief, then, is the bridge between physical presence and internal integration.

It hurts because the bridge is being built.

And bridges require structure.

Time.

Stability.

Support.

Now let us return to the heart of this book.

If love is not lost but adjusted, then grief is the process of learning that adjustment.

You are not trying to erase memory.

You are learning how to hold it without breaking.

You are not trying to replace them.

You are learning how to live while carrying them.

That is a profound human task.

It requires courage.

It requires patience.

It requires allowing yourself to feel without rushing toward explanation.

The world sometimes pressures us to “move on.”

But love does not move on.

It moves inward.

And when it moves inward, it becomes part of your structure.

This is why you can still feel their presence in moments of decision.

Not as a mystical force.

But as integrated wisdom.

Grief does not mean you doubt where they are.

It means you are adjusting to how they now exist in your life.

And that adjustment — though painful — is proof that the bond remains.

You do not grieve what meant nothing.

You grieve what mattered.

And if it mattered enough to hurt…

It matters enough to endure.

Not lost.

Adjusted.

And grief is the sacred work of learning how to live inside that adjustment without losing yourself.

You are not weak for grieving.

You are human.

And being human is the place where love and transformation meet

CHAPTER EIGHT

The Fear of Forgetting — and Why You Will Not

After the sharpness of early grief softens, a new fear sometimes rises.

It is quieter.

Less dramatic.

But deeply unsettling.

What if I forget?

What if their voice fades?

What if their face becomes blurred?

What if one day I cannot remember the exact sound of their laugh?

This fear often surprises people.

They expect grief to be about pain.

They do not expect it to become about preservation.

When someone dies, memory feels like the last remaining bridge.

And when memory shifts — as all memory does — it can feel like a second loss.

But here is something steady and true:

Forgetting details is not the same as losing connection.

The human brain is not designed to store every sensory element with perfect clarity.

It compresses.

It reorganizes.

It simplifies over time.

But emotional imprint remains.

You may not remember the exact pitch of your son's voice in twenty years.

But you will remember how he made you feel.

You may not recall every word your mother ever spoke.

But you will carry the tone of her guidance.

The nervous system does not archive in photographs.

It encodes in influence.

And influence does not fade as quickly as image.

There is also something else to understand.

When we fear forgetting, we are often really fearing disconnection.

We are afraid that if memory softens, the relationship will dissolve.

But relationships do not depend on perfect recall.

They depend on integration.

Ask yourself this:

Have you forgotten the people who shaped you in childhood?

Perhaps you cannot remember every conversation.

But you still move through life shaped by their presence.

That is not forgetting.

That is absorption.

Over time, love becomes less about remembering every detail and more about embodying what was given.

Your father's steadiness becomes your steadiness.

Your child's tenderness becomes your tenderness.

Your neighbor's kindness becomes the way you greet others.

The memory may shift.

But the character remains.

There is something sacred in this transition.

Early grief clings tightly to details.

It revisits photographs.

It replays conversations.

It searches for exactness.

Later grief becomes quieter.

It carries essence rather than image.

And essence is more durable than detail.

Now let us address something gently.

Sometimes people avoid healing because they fear that if the pain softens, the love will diminish.

They hold onto sharp grief as proof of devotion.

But love does not require suffering to remain legitimate.

You are not betraying someone by allowing peace to return.

You are not dishonoring them by laughing again.

You are not forgetting them by building new memories.

Love is not preserved by pain.

It is preserved by integration.

If the pain decreases, it does not mean the bond has weakened.

It means the adjustment is stabilizing.

There is a difference between forgetting and transforming.

Forgetting erases meaning.

Transforming carries meaning forward in new form.

Your relationship with someone who has died will not look like it once did.

It cannot.

But it will not vanish either.

It will change layers.

From conversation to reflection.

From touch to memory.

From presence to influence.

And that influence is not fragile.

It is woven into your nervous system, your values, your habits, your worldview.

Even if one day you cannot remember the exact shape of their handwriting, you will still feel the shape of their love.

And that is what endures.

The fear of forgetting is natural.

But it is unnecessary.

You do not forget what helped build you.

You carry it.

And carrying is not loss.

It is continuation.

Not lost.

Adjusted.

Not erased.

Embedded.

And what is embedded in love does not dissolve quietly with time.

It becomes part of who you are.

Which means, in a very real and grounded way —They continue.

CHAPTER NINE

Signs, Silence, and the Need to Know

At some point in grief, many people begin to look.

Not desperately.

Not irrationally.

But quietly.

They look for signs.

A song that plays at the exact right moment.

A dream that feels unusually vivid.

A sudden memory that arrives with warmth instead of pain.

A coincidence that feels almost intentional.

And beneath the looking is a simple longing:

Let me know you're okay.

Let me know you still exist.

Let me know we are not finished.

This longing is deeply human.

It does not belong to one religion or one spiritual system.

It belongs to attachment.

When someone leaves a room unexpectedly, we call their name.

When someone moves far away, we wait for messages.

When someone dies, we search in subtler ways.

The desire for signs is not foolish.

It is relational continuity seeking reassurance.

But here is where balance becomes essential.

If every small event becomes a message, the mind can become unstable.

If every flicker of light is interpreted as communication, fear can quietly enter.

Healthy comfort feels steady.

Unhealthy searching feels anxious.

There is a difference.

A healthy sense of connection brings calm.

It does not create dependency.

It does not demand constant validation.

It does not require dramatic proof.

It allows quiet.

Sometimes a song plays and you feel warmth.

That warmth may be memory activating attachment pathways.

It may be emotional resonance.

It may be spiritual comfort.

You do not need to label it precisely for it to soothe you.

The comfort is real because the bond was real.

But when silence follows — when no signs appear, when no dreams come — that does not mean absence.

It does not mean abandonment.

It may simply mean that love does not need constant display.

Consider something important.

When your loved one was alive, they were not speaking to you every second.

They were not constantly proving their existence.

The relationship was stable enough to rest.

Perhaps continuity works similarly.

If there is spiritual awareness beyond death, it may not operate through constant interruption of physical reality.

If there is only internal integration, that integration does not require daily symbolic reinforcement.

Either way, silence does not equal disconnection.

Sometimes the need for signs comes from unresolved fear.

Are they suffering?

Are they alone?

Are they unfinished?

Earlier we explored religious traditions, scientific principles, psychological continuity.

Across all of them, one consistent theme emerged:

Transformation, not chaos.

If love shaped order in life, it is unlikely to dissolve into confusion in death.

So when signs are absent, you can rest in something steadier than symbols.

You can rest in what was already proven.

They loved you.

You loved them.

That exchange altered you permanently.

That is not undone by silence.

There is another layer to consider.

The mind is extraordinarily skilled at pattern recognition.

When we are grieving, the brain is heightened.

It scans for reminders.

It connects meaning quickly.

This is not weakness.

It is protective adaptation.

The brain is attempting to restore connection.

But meaning-making does not require supernatural explanation.

It requires emotional honesty.

If a moment brings comfort, receive it.

If it feels forced or obsessive, step back.

The goal is not to collect signs.

The goal is to live steadily.

You are not meant to build your peace on constant external confirmation.

You are meant to build it on integration.

If love continues as influence, you will feel it most clearly not in dramatic signs — but in steady guidance.

In the quiet moment when you make a wise decision.

In the unexpected calm during difficulty.

In the courage that rises when you think you cannot go forward.

Those are not interruptions.

They are internalized strength.

And whether that strength comes from memory, biology, or something beyond — it reflects continuity.

Signs may come.

Silence may come.

Neither determines whether love persists.

Love persists because it already shaped you.

You do not need proof every day.

You need steadiness.

And steadiness grows when you trust that what was real does not require constant validation to remain meaningful.

Not lost.

Not dependent on symbols.

Adjusted.

And living quietly within you, whether the sky sends feathers or not.

CHAPTER TEN

Living Forward Without Leaving Them Behind

There comes a moment in grief when life begins to ask something of you again.

Not harshly.

Not impatiently.

But steadily.

You wake up one morning and realize that the world is still moving.

The sun rises.

Appointments remain.

People need you.

Responsibilities continue.

And beneath all of it, a quiet question forms:

How do I move forward without feeling like I am leaving them behind?

This question carries weight.

Because moving forward can feel like betrayal.

If I laugh again, am I forgetting?

If I build new joy, am I replacing?

If I find peace, am I diminishing what we had?

But forward movement is not abandonment.

It is continuation.

When someone you love dies, your relationship does not end.

It changes position.

It moves from beside you to within you.

You are not walking away from them.

You are walking with what they gave you.

Consider this carefully.

If your son were standing beside you, would he ask you to remain frozen in sorrow?

If your parents could speak clearly, would they want your days to narrow?

If your neighbor could advise you, would she suggest you stop living?

Love does not demand stagnation.

Love strengthens motion.

The healthiest way to honor someone who shaped you is not to stop your life — but to let their influence deepen it.

Living forward does not mean closing the chapter.

It means carrying the chapter into the next one.

The world sometimes frames grief as something to “get over.”

But there is nothing to get over.

There is only something to integrate.

You are not meant to erase the past.

You are meant to expand with it.

And expansion requires movement.

There is also something practical and grounded here.

When you continue living — when you build, serve, create, and love — you are extending the impact of those who shaped you.

Your kindness carries your mother's tone.

Your resilience carries your father's steadiness.

Your tenderness carries your child's softness.

In this way, their story does not stop.

It branches.

Through you.

Forward movement is not separation.

It is multiplication.

You do not leave them behind when you step into new experiences.

You bring them differently.

You bring them as wisdom instead of conversation.

You bring them as strength instead of physical presence.

You bring them as quiet encouragement instead of audible words.

And this shift is not loss.

It is adjustment.

There will be days when forward movement feels natural.

There will be days when it feels heavy.

Both are part of integration.

You are allowed to build new memories.

You are allowed to feel new joy.

You are allowed to experience love again.

None of it diminishes what came before.

Love is not a limited resource.

It does not replace itself.

It expands capacity.

The heart does not close when someone dies.

It stretches.

Sometimes painfully.

But stretching is growth.

And growth does not erase what was planted first.

It grows from it.

At some point, you may notice something subtle.

You are no longer asking every day where they are.

You are no longer searching constantly for signs.

You are living.

Not because you stopped loving.

But because the love has stabilized within you.

That is not forgetting.

That is strength.

Living forward without leaving them behind means trusting this:

What was real cannot be undone.

What shaped you cannot be removed.

What you shared cannot be erased by time.

You do not need to hold onto grief to hold onto them.

You need only to live in a way that reflects what they gave you.

And when you do that —

you are not moving away from them.

You are carrying them forward.

Not lost.

Not left behind.

Adjusted.

And still present in the quiet architecture of who you are becoming.

CHAPTER ELEVEN

The Quiet Architecture of Love

There is something we rarely notice while someone is alive.

Love is building structure.

Not loudly.

Not visibly.

But steadily.

Every shared conversation lays a beam.

Every act of comfort strengthens a wall.

Every conflict resolved reinforces foundation.

Every moment of laughter raises the ceiling a little higher.

We think we are simply living.

But we are constructing.

By the time someone dies, the architecture of your life has already been shaped by their presence.

This is why loss feels destabilizing.

It is not only the absence of a person.

It is the awareness that someone who helped build your internal world is no longer physically here.

And yet — the structure remains.

Your character did not collapse the day they left.

Your values did not dissolve.

Your capacity to love did not vanish.

Because what they built with you is still standing.

This is the quiet architecture of love.

It is not dependent on ongoing physical contact.

It was formed through repetition, influence, and shared experience.

Once formed, it does not disappear.

It holds.

Consider your own life carefully.

The way you speak.

The way you solve conflict.

The way you nurture others.

The way you endure hardship.

These patterns were shaped.

Not randomly.

But relationally.

If your father taught you steadiness, that steadiness now stands inside you.

If your mother modeled compassion, that compassion now frames your interactions.

If your child awakened tenderness, that tenderness now lives in your reflexes.

They are not external to you anymore.

They are structural.

When someone asks, "Where are they now?" we often search for location.

But perhaps a quieter answer is this:

They are in the architecture.

In the beams that hold you upright.

In the wiring that carries your responses.

In the foundation that steadies your decisions.

This is not mystical exaggeration.

It is psychological and relational truth.

No one leaves a deep bond unchanged.

And no deep bond disappears without residue.

The residue is not haunting.

It is shaping.

You may not consciously think of them every day.

But the influence remains active.

When you choose patience over anger, something continues.

When you choose courage over retreat, something continues.

When you offer comfort because you once received it, something continues.

Love becomes architecture when it is repeated long enough.

And architecture does not vanish because the builder steps away.

It remains standing.

This realization can bring unexpected peace.

You do not have to constantly search for signs to know they remain part of your life.

You do not have to prove their presence through symbols.

You can simply observe your own structure.

Notice the resilience you did not always have.

Notice the empathy that deepened through shared experience.

Notice the strength that emerged from shared struggle.

That is continuity.

Not dramatic.

Not mystical.

But steady.

The quiet architecture of love is one of the most enduring forms of presence we know.

It does not require visibility.

It requires recognition.

And when you recognize it, something softens.

You are not alone in your decisions.

You are not unsupported in your character.

You are not starting from nothing.

You are standing in a structure built by years of shared existence.

That structure will carry you forward.

Not because they are physically here — but because what they gave you was integrated deeply enough to hold.

This is another way love adjusts.

It moves from interaction to infrastructure.

From conversation to character.

From shared space to internal stability.

And when you live inside that stability, you are not abandoning them.

You are living within what they helped create.

Not lost.

Not erased.

Built into you.

And architecture built with love does not collapse quietly with time.

It becomes the very frame through which you continue living.

CHAPTER TWELVE

When It Is Your Turn

There is a thought that comes quietly, usually later.

After the funerals.

After the anniversaries.

After the sharpest edges of grief have softened.

If so many I love are now on the unseen side…

One day, I will be too.

This is not a morbid thought.

It is an honest one.

When the population of the unseen begins to outnumber the visible in your personal world, death no longer feels theoretical.

It feels inevitable.

And beneath that awareness is another question:

When it is my turn, what will remain?

We have spent these pages asking where they are.

But now we must gently turn the lens.

What are you building now that will continue when you are no longer physically here?

Because just as their love became architecture in you —

yours is becoming architecture in others.

The way you speak to your grandchildren.

The way you handle disappointment.

The way you forgive.

The way you show up.

All of it is constructing something that will outlive you.

You are someone's internal voice in the making.

You are someone's future resilience.

You are someone's memory that will one day soften grief.

This is not pressure.

It is perspective.

When we understand that love adjusts rather than disappears, fear begins to loosen.

Death becomes less about annihilation and more about transition.

Not a vanishing.

A shifting.

If those who went before you are not lost — only adjusted — then when it is your turn, the same will apply.

Your body will stop.

Your voice will quiet.

Your daily patterns will cease.

But the architecture you built will remain.

The nervous systems you helped regulate will continue.

The courage you modeled will activate in others.

The tenderness you practiced will ripple forward.

You will not evaporate into nothing.

You will reorganize into influence.

This realization changes how we live.

It softens panic.

It steadies anxiety.

It reminds us that what we are doing now matters beyond the moment.

We do not control the timing of our departure.

But we shape the quality of what we leave behind.

And what we leave behind is not only property or possessions.

It is tone.

It is memory.

It is character.

It is love expressed repeatedly enough to become structural.

There is something peaceful in this.

If love continues in adjusted form, then death is not an enemy of meaning.

It is part of the cycle of integration.

You received architecture from those before you.

You are now building architecture for those who will remain.

This does not remove the sadness of eventual departure.

But it removes the terror of erasure.

You will not be erased.

You will be adjusted.

Just as they were.

And perhaps, when it is your turn, the fear will be less because you have already watched love survive on the other side.

You have already seen influence persist.

You have already felt the structure hold.

So when your time comes, you will not step into emptiness.

You will step into transformation.

And those who remain will ask where you are.

And they will discover — in their steadiness, in their strength, in their quiet architecture — that you are not lost.

Only adjusted.

Just as love has always been.

CHAPTER THIRTEEN

The Unseen Is Not Empty

There is one final fear that often hides beneath all the others.

Not just, *Where are they?*

Not just, *Do they continue?*

Not just, *Will I forget?*

But something more primal:

What if the unseen is empty?

What if all of this longing is reaching into nothing?

It is a question many people are afraid to say out loud.

Because to ask it feels like doubt.

But asking is not disbelief.

It is honesty.

And honesty deserves steadiness, not shame.

Let us approach this calmly.

If the unseen were empty — if death were absolute erasure — then love would be the most irrational force in existence.

Because love demands investment.

It demands vulnerability.

It demands time.

It demands sacrifice.

And yet human beings across all cultures and centuries continue to love deeply, even knowing death is inevitable.

Why?

Because something in us resists the idea that meaning collapses into nothingness.

Even the most secular perspectives acknowledge this:

When someone dies, their impact continues.

Their work continues.

Their influence continues.

Their imprint continues.

An empty unseen would require a universe in which meaning has no endurance.

But endurance is written into the structure of reality.

Stars collapse and become new stars.

Forests burn and become soil for future growth.

Energy transforms.

Systems reorganize.

Nothing in nature suggests annihilation without residue.

So why would love — the most complex and transformative force we know — be the single exception?

The unseen may be mysterious.

But mystery is not emptiness.

There are entire layers of reality we cannot perceive with the human eye.

Radio frequencies fill the air.

Microscopic organisms shape ecosystems.

Dark matter composes much of the universe.

We do not see them.

But we do not conclude they are not there.

We simply acknowledge limitation.

When it comes to death, humility is essential.

We do not possess full understanding.

But lack of full understanding is not proof of absence.

It is proof of boundary.

The unseen is not empty.

It is simply beyond current measurement.

And even if someone holds the belief that consciousness ends at death, something still remains undeniable:

Love reshapes those who remain.

If love continues in the living, then meaning continues.

If meaning continues, then the story does not collapse.

And if the story does not collapse, then existence is not wasted.

Whether the unseen is a dimension of consciousness, a spiritual realm, a transformed energetic field, or a mystery we cannot yet articulate —

it is not nothing.

Because nothing does not produce enduring influence.

Nothing does not shape character.

Nothing does not leave architecture behind.

The fact that you still feel the depth of what was shared is itself evidence of continuation in some form.

Not dramatic continuation.

Not theatrical continuation.

But steady.

You are living proof that the relationship mattered.

And if it mattered, it altered reality.

Reality does not revert to zero.

Now let us return to something simpler.

When you stand quietly and think of those you love who have passed, what do you feel?

Chaos?

Or depth?

Panic?

Or weight?

For most people, there is sadness — yes.

But also something steady.

A gravity.

A significance.

That gravity is not emptiness.

It is presence in adjusted form.

The unseen is not a void.

It is a layer.

A layer that holds memory, influence, transformation, and possibly consciousness in ways we are still learning to understand.

You do not have to define it fully.

You do not have to map it precisely.

You only need to recognize that love does not behave like nothing.

It behaves like something enduring.

And enduring forces do not dissolve into emptiness without trace.

They adjust.

They reorganize.

They continue in ways both measurable and mysterious.

The unseen is not empty.

It is simply unseen.

And unseen does not mean absent.

It means we are still growing into the ability to understand it.

Not lost.

Not erased.

Not vanished into nothing.

Adjusted.

Held in a dimension of continuity that may be quieter than we expect — but no less real.

CHAPTER FOURTEEN

Guarded by Light

After all the questions…

After the theology, the science, the psychology…

After the searching and the adjusting…

There remains something quieter.

Not an answer.

But a steadiness.

You may not know the precise structure of the afterlife.

You may not be able to define exactly where your loved ones are.

You may not receive daily signs or dramatic reassurance.

And yet —

You are not unraveling.

You are not collapsing.

You are living.

There is something holding you.

Call it faith.

Call it integration.

Call it nervous system adaptation.

Call it grace.

But it is real.

You have walked through loss that once felt impossible.

You have stood in kitchens that felt too quiet.

You have passed birthdays that no longer include certain voices.

You have survived days you once believed you could not endure.

And still —

You are here.

This is not accidental.

This is architecture holding.

This is love stabilizing.

This is adjustment becoming strength.

To be “guarded by light” does not mean you are protected from sorrow.

It does not mean you are shielded from death.

It does not mean you avoid grief.

It means that through sorrow, something luminous remains intact.

Something in you refuses collapse.

Something in you continues to trust that love was not meaningless.

Something in you understands — even without complete explanation — that what you shared has not dissolved into nothing.

The light that guards you is not theatrical.

It is not dramatic intervention.

It is quiet resilience.

It is the ability to remember without breaking.

It is the ability to move forward without abandoning.

It is the ability to love again without diminishing what was.

You are guarded by the very love that once flowed between you.

That love now lives inside your decisions.

Inside your patience.

Inside your courage.

Inside your softened edges.

You may not see your loved ones walking beside you.

But you walk with what they built.

You may not hear their voice in the air.

But you hear its echo in your conscience.

You may not know the geography of the unseen.

But you know the weight of what mattered.

And that weight does not vanish.

It steadies you.

There will still be days of ache.

There will still be moments of longing.

But beneath those waves, something solid remains.

You are not standing on emptiness.

You are standing on continuation.

The unseen world may hold more names now than the visible one.

But the visible world still holds you.

And you are living proof that love does not disappear.

It adjusts.

It reorganizes.

It transforms into guidance, into architecture, into strength.

And when your time eventually comes — as it will for all of us — you will not step into nothing.

You will step into the same mystery that now holds those you love.

And just as you were guarded by the light of what they gave you — someone will one day be guarded by the light you leave behind.

This is not fantasy.

It is the most grounded truth we have uncovered:

Love alters reality.

Altered reality does not revert to zero.

It continues.

Not lost.

Not erased.

Adjusted.

And in that adjustment, there is light.

And in that light, there is steadiness.

And in that steadiness — there is peace.

PART II – BEYOND THE VEIL

CHAPTER FIFTEEN

Beyond Survival — Does Growth Continue?

Up to this point, we have asked whether love survives.

Now we must ask something deeper.

If it survives…

Does it remain unchanged?

Or does it continue to grow?

Life, as we experience it here, is developmental.

A child becomes an adult.

Ignorance becomes understanding.

Fear becomes wisdom.

Pain becomes compassion.

Growth is written into our earthly experience.

We mature emotionally.

We expand intellectually.

We deepen spiritually.

So here is a reasonable question:

Why would development suddenly stop at death?

If consciousness continues in any form — whether as soul, awareness, or transformed energy — would it freeze in its final earthly condition?

Or would it continue evolving?

Many religious traditions suggest continuation is not static.

Christian theology speaks of sanctification and fullness in the presence of God — not stagnation.

Eastern philosophies speak of ongoing cycles of learning.

Mystical traditions across cultures describe expansion of awareness beyond bodily limitation.

Even near-death accounts often describe increased clarity rather than suspension.

No serious tradition describes the afterlife as a permanent waiting room of inactivity.

The language differs.

But the theme is consistent:

Transformation continues.

Now let us approach this rationally.

While alive, our growth is often limited by:

Fear.

Ego.

Physical pain.

Biological impulse.

Time constraints.

If death releases us from bodily limitation, then perhaps it also releases us from certain distortions.

Not erasing personality — but refining essence.

Consider this carefully.

Your loved one was not only their habits.

They were not only their flaws.

They were not only their moments of weakness.

There was something deeper — something essential — that you loved.

That essence is what bonded you.

If growth continues beyond physical life, perhaps what continues growing is essence — not ego.

Perhaps impatience softens.

Perhaps misunderstanding clarifies.

Perhaps pain dissolves into comprehension.

This is not wishful thinking.

It is consistent with the developmental pattern we observe in life.

We do not mature in order to stop maturing.

Growth appears to be a principle, not a phase.

Now let us consider something else.

If those who passed before us continue evolving, then the unseen is not static.

It is active.

Not chaotic.

Not crowded.

But structured.

Just as this life has seasons, perhaps the unseen has stages.

Rest.

Reflection.

Integration.

Expansion.

Earlier we asked where they are.

Perhaps a more meaningful question is:

What are they becoming?

If they are free from physical pain, then perhaps clarity increases.

If they are free from time, then perhaps perspective expands.

If they are free from fear, then perhaps love deepens without distortion.

And if love deepens there…

Then our bond with them is not anchored in who they were at their most limited — but in who they are becoming at their most refined.

This changes grief.

It shifts the image from loss to transition.

Not that we stop missing them.

But that we understand they are not frozen in their final struggle.

They are not suspended in illness.

They are not trapped in weakness.

If continuation includes growth, then they are not diminished.

They are progressing.

And this possibility introduces something powerful.

If they are growing…

And we are growing…

Then perhaps relationship does not end.

It changes frequency.

Not communication as we once knew it.

But resonance.

We evolve here through experience.

Perhaps they evolve there through integration.

Both movements are forward.

Not lost.

Not paused.

Not stalled in eternity.

But developing.

This chapter does not claim certainty.

It asks a reasonable question based on observable patterns:

If growth defines life, why assume growth ends?

Perhaps death is not the termination of development.

Perhaps it is the continuation of it in a different dimension of awareness.

And if that is true, then the unseen is not a museum of the past.

It is a field of ongoing becoming.

And that means the ones you love are not fixed in memory alone.

They are still unfolding.

Just as you are.

And unfolding is not extinction.

It is evolution.

CHAPTER SIXTEEN

Recognition — Will We Know Them Again?

If growth continues…

If essence refines…

If consciousness expands…

Then another question naturally follows:

If we meet again — will we recognize one another?

This question is not sentimental.

It is structural.

Because love is not abstract.

It is relational.

When you think of those you have lost, you do not think of anonymous souls.

You think of specific faces.

Specific voices.

Specific gestures.

You remember the way your son tilted his head when he laughed.

The tone your mother used when she corrected you gently.

The steady presence of your father in a room.

Love attaches to identity.

So when we consider continuation beyond death, we must ask:

Does identity remain?

Or does it dissolve into something impersonal?

Across religious traditions, recognition is assumed.

Christian teachings describe reunion.

Jewish tradition speaks of gathering.

Islamic theology describes awareness.

Eastern traditions speak of karmic connection across lifetimes.

Though the frameworks differ, relational continuity appears again and again.

Even in near-death accounts, individuals often describe recognizing loved ones — not through facial features alone, but through immediate knowing.

Recognition seems less about appearance and more about essence.

Now let us approach this rationally.

What is identity?

Is it the body?

The body changes every few years at the cellular level.

Is it personality?

Personality evolves throughout life.

Is it memory?

Memory fades, alters, and reconstructs.

And yet something consistent remains.

There is a core sense of "I."

Even as your body aged…

Even as your beliefs matured…

Even as your experiences reshaped you…

You remained you.

Not identical to your younger self — but continuous.

Identity, then, may not be a fixed image.

It may be a through-line.

An organizing coherence.

If consciousness continues beyond physical life, perhaps that organizing coherence continues as well.

Not frozen at a specific age.

Not limited by illness.

Not restricted by bodily form.

But recognizable through essence.

Consider something simple.

Even now, when you hear someone's voice on the phone, you recognize them instantly.

Not because you see their face.

But because tone carries identity.

Identity is frequency as much as form.

We already recognize people by energy, by rhythm, by the way they enter a room.

So if recognition exists beyond physical structure, it may operate through essence rather than appearance.

Now let us consider growth again.

If those who passed continue evolving, they may not remain exactly as they were at their final earthly moment.

If someone died in illness, perhaps that illness no longer defines them.

If someone struggled with fear, perhaps fear no longer distorts their clarity.

Would that make them unrecognizable?

Or would it make them more fully themselves?

You loved your child not because of his limitations — but because of his essence.

You loved your parents not because of their aging bodies — but because of their presence.

If essence refines beyond bodily limitation, then recognition may deepen rather than disappear.

There is something else to consider.

Human relationships create imprint.

Shared experience forms resonance.

When two people love deeply, they develop attunement.

They sense one another's emotional shifts.

They anticipate one another's needs.

They feel comfort in one another's presence.

That attunement is not erased by death.

It is integrated.

If consciousness continues, then perhaps relational attunement continues as well.

Not as constant observation.

Not as physical proximity.

But as recognition of shared history.

Now let us move carefully into something important.

If reunion occurs — if recognition happens — it is unlikely to be a return to earthly dynamics exactly as they were.

Growth changes perspective.

Imagine meeting someone again without ego defensiveness.

Without misunderstanding.

Without physical limitation.

Without the distortions of time pressure.

Recognition would not be regression.

It would be clarity.

You would not meet as you were in conflict.

You would meet as you are in understanding.

This possibility reframes longing.

You are not hoping to reclaim the past exactly as it was.

You are hoping to experience love without distortion.

And that is not childish.

It is deeply human.

Now let us remain grounded.

We cannot measure reunion.

We cannot map it scientifically.

But we can observe this:

Human intuition across cultures consistently assumes recognition.

That persistence is meaningful.

It suggests that relational continuity is not merely theological invention — but something embedded in our psychological structure.

Why would humans instinctively expect recognition if connection were purely temporary?

The expectation itself may point toward continuity.

At minimum, it reveals how deeply relational identity is.

We do not exist as isolated individuals.

We exist through connection.

And connection creates imprint that does not dissolve easily.

If growth continues beyond physical life…

If essence refines rather than disappears…

If consciousness is more fundamental than we fully understand…

Then recognition is not unreasonable.

Not as frozen personalities repeating old patterns.

But as matured essences meeting in clarity.

This does not remove the ache of missing them now.

But it changes the shape of hope.

Hope becomes less about reclaiming what was — and more about trusting that what was real is not lost.

It is unfolding.

And if unfolding continues on both sides of the veil…

Then perhaps recognition is not only possible.

It is natural.

Not sentimental fantasy.

Not wishful thinking.

But the logical extension of continuity.

You are not loving into emptiness.

You are loving into mystery.

And mystery does not negate relationship.

It expands it.

If growth continues…

If essence refines…

If love reorganizes rather than collapses…

Then recognition may be less about seeing the same face —

and more about knowing the same soul.

And knowing has always been deeper than sight.

Not lost.

Not erased.

Becoming.

And perhaps — one day — recognized again in fuller clarity than we have ever known here.

CHAPTER SEVENTEEN

The Veil Is Not a Wall

There is a common image people carry about death.

A door slamming shut.

A curtain dropping.

A wall rising between worlds.

The living on one side.

The dead on the other.

Separation complete.

But what if the veil is not a wall?

What if it is a threshold?

A membrane.

A shift in density.

A change in frequency.

Not a barricade.

A transition.

We already live in layers of reality we cannot see.

Radio waves pass through your body at this very moment.

Microscopic life thrives on surfaces that appear empty.

The universe itself is composed largely of matter we cannot directly observe.

Invisible does not mean nonexistent.

It means beyond current perception.

When we speak of a “veil,” we often imagine fabric — thin but opaque.

But perhaps the veil is more like water.

When you stand above a lake, you cannot see deeply into it unless the surface is still.

Movement distorts visibility.

Calm clarifies.

Perhaps the boundary between dimensions is not sealed.

Perhaps it is simply beyond the range of ordinary sensory awareness.

This is where the conversation becomes enchanting — not because it abandons reason, but because it stretches it.

Consider consciousness.

Even now, your awareness can travel instantly.

You can think of a childhood memory and be emotionally present in it.

You can imagine a place thousands of miles away.

You can dream vividly while your body remains motionless.

Your mind already transcends physical location in certain states.

So what changes at death?

Does consciousness cease entirely?

Or does it shift into a state where physical sensory input is no longer required?

If the latter is even remotely possible, then the veil is not a prison.

It is a change in interface.

You are currently operating through a body.

Perhaps beyond death, consciousness operates differently.

Less limited by time.

Less confined by space.

Less burdened by biological impulse.

This does not mean omniscience.

It does not mean godlike power.

It means adjustment of perception.

Now imagine something quietly beautiful.

If physical senses are removed, perhaps awareness becomes more refined.

Without pain, clarity increases.

Without fear, perception steadies.

Without ego defensiveness, understanding expands.

You loved the essence of those you lost — not merely their bodies.

If essence continues, perhaps it becomes more luminous.

Not glowing theatrically.

But clarified.

Purified of distortion.

Freed from the heaviness of survival instinct.

This reframes something profound.

When you miss them, you are missing their physical accessibility.

But their essence may not be diminished.

It may be more whole than ever.

And if growth continues — as we explored — then they are not suspended in the moment of their final breath.

They are not trapped in illness.

They are not frozen in age.

They are moving.

Expanding.

Integrating.

Becoming.

This possibility does not remove grief.

But it infuses it with awe.

The veil, then, is not a dividing line between existence and nothingness.

It is a threshold between density and refinement.

Between weight and lightness.

Between time-bound experience and expanded awareness.

Now let us move into something even more enchanting.

What if the veil works both ways — not in constant communication, not in dramatic interruption — but in resonance?

When you feel sudden strength in a moment of weakness…

When unexpected calm enters grief…

When clarity arises without explanation…

You do not need to conclude supernatural intervention.

But you can consider this:

If love reorganizes into influence…

If consciousness is not strictly confined to physical measurement…

If essence continues evolving…

Then resonance is not impossible.

Not voices in the room.

Not figures at the foot of the bed.

But alignment.

A tuning.

Just as two instruments tuned to the same frequency vibrate sympathetically.

You are already carrying their architecture.

If they continue evolving in essence, perhaps that resonance deepens rather than fades.

Not constant.

Not intrusive.

But present as shared coherence.

And here is where excitement rises — not childish excitement, but sacred anticipation.

If death is transition rather than extinction…

If growth continues…

If recognition is possible…

If the veil is permeable in principle…

Then existence is far more layered than we assumed.

Life becomes preparation.

Not preparation for judgment in fear.

But preparation for expansion.

Every act of love here builds capacity there.

Every act of forgiveness here refines essence there.

Every act of courage here strengthens coherence there.

This is not superstition.

It is the logical extension of continuity.

If development defines life…

If development continues…

Then this life is not isolated.

It is part of a larger unfolding.

You are not simply surviving until an ending.

You are participating in an arc.

An arc that may extend beyond the visible chapter.

The veil, then, is not terrifying.

It is mysterious.

And mystery is not the enemy of peace.

It is the birthplace of wonder.

You do not need to know the mechanics.

You only need to recognize the pattern.

Nothing in nature supports annihilation without transformation.

Nothing in love supports meaninglessness.

Nothing in growth supports sudden cessation without continuation.

So when you think of those you love beyond the veil, do not imagine them confined to shadow.

Imagine them freed from distortion.

Imagine them continuing in clarity.

Imagine them expanding into fuller expression of who they truly are.

Not lost.

Not dimmed.

Not reduced.

Refined.

And when your time eventually comes, the veil will not be a wall.

It will be a crossing.

Not into darkness.

But into a dimension where what was always unseen becomes visible in new form.

Exciting?

Yes.

Because existence may be far more magnificent than fear ever allowed.

Enchanting?

Yes.

Because love may be far more durable than death ever suggested.

You are not living in a fragile universe.

You are living in a layered one.

And layers do not negate one another.

They deepen the whole.

The veil is not a wall.

It is a threshold.

And thresholds are not endings.

They are passages.

Not lost.

Not severed.

Becoming.

And perhaps — beyond sight — becoming in ways more radiant than we have yet imagined.

CHAPTER EIGHTEEN

Time Is Not What We Think

There is something we have not yet questioned.

We assume death separates us because we assume time separates us.

They died "before" us.

We are still here "after" them.

One day we will go "later."

But what if time is not as rigid as it feels?

Physics has already revealed something astonishing:

Time is not constant.

It bends.

It stretches.

It behaves differently depending on gravity and velocity.

Under certain conditions, time slows.

Under others, it accelerates.

Einstein showed us that time is woven into space — not a fixed ticking clock above the universe.

If time itself is flexible within the physical universe…

What happens when consciousness is no longer confined to the body?

We experience time linearly because our bodies require sequence.

We wake.

We age.

We move moment by moment.

But even now, your mind does not obey strict time.

You can relive childhood in seconds.

You can imagine the future vividly.

In dreams, hours pass in minutes.

Your consciousness already moves differently than your clock.

So here is the question that changes everything:

If those who have passed are no longer bound to biological time, do they experience separation the way we do?

To us, years may pass.

To them — if they are in a state beyond linear sequence — there may be no "waiting."

No distance measured in decades.

No aging.

No sense of being left behind.

Imagine this carefully.

If time bends within the universe…

And consciousness is not fully explained by biology…

Then death may not feel like separation from their perspective.

It may feel like continuity.

We experience absence because we are still inside the sequence.

But from a dimension not bound to sequence, what we call "later" may not exist.

This is not mystical invention.

It is a philosophical extension of relativity.

Time is relative to the observer.

If the observer changes state, the experience of time changes.

This reframes longing.

You feel the ache of missing them over years.

But if they are not bound to linear time, reunion may not feel delayed.

It may feel immediate when it occurs.

There may be no sensation of waiting.

No sense of abandonment.

Only transition.

This possibility removes something heavy.

It removes the image of them somewhere counting time without you.

It removes the fear that they are suspended in endless waiting.

If consciousness continues outside biological constraint, time may not function as we assume.

And if time does not function as we assume, separation may not either.

Now let us step further — carefully.

If time is flexible…

And growth continues…

And essence refines…

Then the arc of existence may not be a straight line.

It may be layered.

Simultaneous in ways we cannot perceive from within the sequence.

You experience your life as a timeline.

But perhaps from a broader perspective, your entire existence — past, present, future — is visible at once.

Just as you can see an entire landscape from above that cannot be seen from within a forest.

This does not eliminate free will.

It does not eliminate responsibility.

It expands context.

The veil may not divide two distant places.

It may divide two vantage points.

From here, you see through time.

From there, perhaps time is seen as whole.

This is why reunion might not feel like reclaiming something lost in duration.

It may feel like stepping into a continuity that never truly fractured.

Exciting?

Yes.

Because it suggests something breathtaking:

Love may not be stretched thin across decades.

It may exist in a dimension where separation is a perspective, not a permanent condition.

You are still living inside the sequence.

They may not be.

And that difference changes how absence feels.

It does not erase your grief.

But it reframes eternity.

Eternity may not be endless future time.

It may be freedom from time.

And freedom from time changes everything.

It means no decay.

No rushing.

No running out.

No waiting rooms.

Just presence in another mode.

If this is even partially true, then the veil is not a distance measured in years.

It is a shift in dimension.

And dimensions are not farther away.

They are differently structured.

This chapter does not claim certainty.

It opens possibility grounded in physics and philosophy.

If time bends…

If consciousness transcends physical measurement…

If growth continues beyond bodily limitation…

Then separation is not what we think.

You are not loving across a canyon of endless years.

You are loving across a shift in perception.

And perception is not permanent.

Not lost.

Not abandoned in time.

Not drifting through decades alone.

Adjusted.

Perhaps in a dimension where time does not wound the way it does here.

Perhaps in a state where reunion is not delayed — only unseen from this side.

And that is not only comforting.

It is magnificent.

Because it suggests that love is not trapped inside clocks.

It moves beyond them.

And if love is not bound by time…

Then neither is connection.

The veil is not measured in years.

It is measured in awareness.

And awareness is always expanding.

CHAPTER NINETEEN

The Purpose of Passage

We often think of death as interruption.

A life cut short.

A conversation unfinished.

A story halted mid-sentence.

But what if death is not interruption?

What if it is transition within a larger design?

Nature does not waste process.

Seeds fall into soil and disappear before they rise again.

Stars collapse before becoming something new.

Caterpillars dissolve inside cocoons before emerging transformed.

In every visible system, passage precedes transformation.

We accept this in biology.

We accept it in physics.

We struggle to accept it in ourselves.

Why?

Because we are attached to form.

We want the voice, the hands, the familiar gestures.

But form is not the only dimension of life.

Essence may be the deeper one.

If passage exists throughout nature as part of growth, then death may not be anomaly.

It may be continuity within a greater arc.

Let us ask something bold but rational:

If consciousness continues, why?

If growth extends beyond physical life, toward what?

Is it rest?

Is it refinement?

Is it reunion?

Is it preparation for another stage of existence?

Across spiritual traditions, one idea appears repeatedly:

Life has purpose beyond survival.

Christianity speaks of eternal life not as mere duration, but as fullness.

Eastern traditions speak of liberation and awakening.

Mystical traditions speak of union with greater awareness.

Even philosophical humanism suggests that meaning extends beyond individual lifespan through influence.

Every framework implies trajectory.

Forward movement.

Not stagnation.

If life here is developmental — if we learn through love, loss, forgiveness, courage — then perhaps this life is preparatory.

Not in fear-based judgment.

But in expansion-based growth.

Every act of compassion deepens us.

Every hardship endured reshapes us.

Every forgiveness practiced refines us.

These are not random events.

They are formative.

If nothing were beyond this life, growth would culminate abruptly.

But growth does not feel abrupt.

It feels progressive.

Layered.

Incomplete at the moment of death.

So what if death is not cancellation of growth — but continuation of it in different terrain?

What if passage has purpose?

Not punishment.

Not escape.

But progression.

Now allow this idea to settle.

The people you love who have passed may not simply be "resting."

They may be integrating.

Integrating experience.

Clarifying lessons.

Expanding understanding beyond bodily limitation.

This does not mean they are busy in human terms.

It means consciousness may not be idle.

Growth does not require physical movement.

It requires awareness.

And awareness may be clearer without biological noise.

Imagine a state where misunderstanding dissolves.

Where regret transforms into comprehension.

Where love is no longer obstructed by insecurity.

If growth continues, then death is not an ending.

It is a phase shift.

And if passage has purpose, then grief, though painful, is part of something meaningful.

You are not watching loved ones disappear into randomness.

You are witnessing transition into deeper becoming.

This reframes your own life.

You are not merely enduring time until you die.

You are developing.

Every choice matters.

Every love matters.

Every act of integrity strengthens the architecture of who you are becoming.

And if becoming does not stop at death…

Then this life is sacred training ground.

Not in fear.

In magnificence.

This does not remove sorrow.

But it transforms despair into awe.

If passage has purpose, then death is not enemy of meaning.

It is doorway within it.

And if that is true…

Then when you stand at the edge of loss, you are not staring into collapse.

You are standing at a threshold in a universe that favors transformation over annihilation.

Exciting?

Yes.

Because it suggests that existence is not accidental.

Enchanting?

Yes.

Because it implies that love is not fragile.

You are not living in a universe that wastes souls.

You are living in one that refines them.

Not lost.

Not halted.

Not erased.

Passing through.

And passage is not termination.

It is movement.

Movement into greater clarity.

Movement into fuller awareness.

Movement into expanded light.

And if passage has purpose…

Then love has trajectory.

And trajectory means we are all moving somewhere — not into nothing — but into more.

And more is not frightening.

It is breathtaking.

CHAPTER TWENTY

Love Is the Constant

Everything changes.

Bodies change.

Ages change.

Seasons change.

Forms change.

Time bends.

Consciousness shifts.

But one thing has remained consistent through every chapter of this exploration:

Love does not disappear.

It transforms.

It reorganizes.

It refines.

It deepens.

But it does not vanish.

This is not sentimental thinking.

It is observable.

Love alters brain chemistry.

Love reshapes nervous systems.

Love builds architecture in personality.

Love motivates sacrifice.

Love outlives the body in influence.

Nothing else in human experience behaves this way.

Anger fades.

Fear shifts.

Desires evolve.

Possessions decay.

Love, when real, integrates.

It becomes structural.

And structural forces are not easily undone.

Now let us expand this beyond human psychology.

The universe itself appears relational.

Particles interact.

Fields influence one another.

Systems form through attraction and resonance.

At its most basic level, existence is interaction.

And interaction produces connection.

Connection produces coherence.

Coherence produces structure.

Love may be the highest human expression of this universal principle.

It binds.

It harmonizes.

It organizes.

So when a body dies, the organizing principle does not collapse.

The form that expressed it changes.

But the binding force remains active.

This is why you still feel shaped.

This is why memory carries weight.

This is why influence persists.

Love behaves like a constant within changing conditions.

In mathematics, constants anchor equations.

In physics, constants stabilize reality.

Perhaps love is a constant in consciousness.

Everything else is variable.

Age is variable.

Health is variable.

Circumstance is variable.

Duration is variable.

Love remains.

Not always in intensity.

Not always in expression.

But in essence.

If growth continues beyond death…

If consciousness expands…

If time is flexible…

If passage has purpose…

Then love is not merely something we experience here.

It may be something we are moving toward more fully.

Perhaps this life is practice in loving through limitation.

Learning to love imperfectly.

Learning to forgive through ego.

Learning to care through vulnerability.

If limitation falls away beyond the veil…

Then what remains may be love in clarified form.

Not possessive.

Not fearful.

Not attached to control.

But coherent.

Pure.

Aligned.

This is enchanting — not because it is fantasy — but because it suggests that the deepest thing you have ever felt is not temporary.

When you held your child for the first time, that love was not random chemistry.

It was binding force.

When you forgave someone who hurt you, that love was not weakness.

It was structural strength.

When you grieved deeply, that love was not misplaced.

It was evidence of permanence.

If love is the constant, then death does not interrupt it.

It removes certain variables.

But the constant remains.

And if love is constant…

Then reunion, growth, recognition, and passage are not separate themes.

They are expressions of the same force unfolding across dimensions.

This is where fear begins to lose power.

You are not standing at the mercy of chaos.

You are living inside a universe where connection shapes reality.

Love shaped you.

Love shaped them.

Love will shape what comes next.

Not sentimentally.

Structurally.

And if love is the constant, then nothing you have shared is wasted.

Not a single embrace.

Not a single tear.

Not a single word spoken in tenderness.

Constants do not dissolve.

They anchor.

You are anchored.

They are anchored.

Not to form.

But to essence.

And essence is not fragile.

It is the most enduring layer of identity.

So when you ask, in quiet moments, "Are they truly gone?"

You can answer gently:

The form is gone.

The love is not.

And if love is the constant —

then nothing essential has been erased.

It has only shifted expression.

Not lost.

Not severed.

Not reduced to memory alone.

Becoming.

Expanding.

Remaining.

Love is the constant.

And constants do not disappear when variables change.

They remain the foundation of the equation.

And you are still living inside that equation —

held by the same force that first taught you how to love.

PART IV – BECOMING

CHAPTER TWENTY-ONE

We Are Becoming More Than We Were

There is something subtle that happens after deep loss.

At first, you feel smaller.

Quieter.

Hollowed.

Reduced.

But if you look carefully — months later, years later — you may notice something unexpected.

You are not smaller.

You are deeper.

Grief enlarges capacity.

It stretches perception.

It softens judgment.

It refines priorities.

The person who has loved and lost is not diminished.

They are expanded.

This is not romanticizing pain.

It is recognizing transformation.

Before loss, life often feels surface-bound.

Schedules.

Obligations.

Routines.

After loss, reality feels layered.

You sense fragility.

You sense sacredness.

You sense time differently.

You speak more carefully.

You love more deliberately.

You forgive more urgently.

Why?

Because loss revealed something essential:

Nothing physical is permanent.

But what is built in love endures.

That realization changes you.

You begin to live less casually.

Less distracted.

More aware.

You are becoming more than you were.

Loss has refined you.

This is where enchantment returns — not whimsical enchantment, but sacred awe.

What if grief itself is part of evolution?

What if the stretching of the heart is not damage —

but expansion?

The heart that has been broken open does not close back the same way.

It holds more.

More compassion.

More humility.

More patience.

You begin to see others differently.

You recognize pain in strangers.

You recognize longing in silence.

You recognize that everyone is carrying someone on the unseen side.

The world becomes more connected.

Not less.

You become more connected.

And this matters.

Because if love is the constant…

And growth continues…

And passage has purpose…

Then grief is not interruption of life.

It is acceleration of depth.

You are not simply surviving loss.

You are being shaped by it.

Just as those who passed shaped you in life…

Their absence now shapes you in new ways.

You are becoming more courageous.

More thoughtful.

More anchored in what matters.

This is not accidental.

It is the natural consequence of loving deeply.

The more deeply you love, the more deeply you grow.

Even through pain.

Especially through pain.

Now let us widen this.

If those who passed continue evolving…

And you continue evolving…

Then love is not only constant.

It is developmental.

It stretches both sides.

You refine here.

They refine there.

You are not moving in opposite directions.

You are both expanding.

And expansion creates capacity for greater recognition, greater clarity, greater coherence.

This is exciting.

Because it means existence is not shrinking.

It is enlarging.

You are not approaching a narrowing end.

You are approaching a widening horizon.

The more you love, the more capable you become of deeper love.

The more you forgive, the more capable you become of peace.

The more you endure, the more capable you become of strength.

Loss did not reduce your capacity.

It increased it.

You are becoming more than you were before you lost them.

Not because you wanted this path.

But because love does not allow stagnation.

It moves.

It grows.

It refines.

And if this pattern holds true beyond death…

Then becoming does not stop at the veil.

It continues.

You are not moving toward less.

You are moving toward more.

More awareness.

More coherence.

More alignment.

More love without distortion.

This chapter is not about them.

It is about you.

You are not who you were before grief.

You are deeper.

And depth is not weakness.

It is expansion.

Expansion prepares you.

Not for fear.

But for magnificence.

If passage has purpose…

If time bends…

If love is constant…

If growth continues…

Then you are not drifting toward extinction.

You are evolving toward greater fullness.

The ones you love are not ahead of you in absence.

They may be ahead of you in clarity.

And you are moving toward that clarity too.

Not rushing.

Not forced.

But unfolding.

You are becoming more than you were.

And becoming is not loss.

It is transformation.

Not smaller.

Not hollow.

Expanded.

And expansion is the language of a universe that does not waste love — but grows it.

And you are part of that growth.

CHAPTER TWENTY-TWO

The Memory of Home

There is a feeling that sometimes rises in quiet moments.

It is not grief.

It is not fear.

It is not even longing exactly.

It is something deeper.

A sense that you have known something before.

A sense that this life, as real as it is, is not the whole of your existence.

A subtle awareness that you are familiar with something beyond words.

Many people describe it differently.

Some call it spiritual homesickness.

Some call it divine longing.

Some call it eternity placed in the heart.

It feels like remembering without specific memory.

Like recognizing without image.

Like belonging to something larger than the visible world.

Where does that come from?

If human beings were purely accidental biological events, why would we carry a persistent sense of transcendence?

Why would we intuit depth beyond what we can measure?

Why would loss awaken not only sadness — but a strange sense of something sacred?

Perhaps because somewhere within us is the memory of home.

Not a physical house.

Not a childhood address.

But a state of coherence.

A state of belonging without separation.

A state where love is not strained by time or distance.

When someone we love dies, that memory intensifies.

Not because we want to escape life.

But because something inside us recognizes continuity.

We do not mourn like beings who believe in nothing.

We mourn like beings who sense more.

Even those who claim no religious belief often speak in the language of transcendence when confronted with death.

"She's at peace."

"He's free now."

"They're together again."

These phrases rise instinctively.

As though the heart refuses annihilation as a final answer.

This is not denial.

It is intuition.

Intuition is not proof.

But it is pattern recognition beneath conscious reasoning.

You may have felt it yourself.

In certain quiet moments — perhaps at dusk, perhaps alone — you sense that existence is layered.

That you are not just a body moving through years.

That you belong to something wider.

That life feels like a chapter, not the entire book.

This is enchanting — not because it is vague, but because it is persistent.

The memory of home may not be specific.

But it is steady.

It surfaces in music.

In beauty.

In moments of profound love.

In silence.

And especially in grief.

Loss tears open the illusion that this world is permanent.

And when that illusion breaks, something else becomes visible.

Not emptiness.

Depth.

You begin to sense that this life may not be the origin of your being — nor its conclusion.

If growth continues…

If passage has purpose…

If love is constant…

If time bends…

Then perhaps existence stretches beyond this visible interval.

And if it stretches, then home may not be behind you or ahead of you.

It may be beneath you.

The foundation of your being.

The place from which you emerged.

The place to which you return.

Not in regression.

In completion.

This does not mean abandoning life here.

It means living here with deeper awareness.

You are not a stranger in this world.

But you are not entirely confined to it either.

You carry the memory of coherence.

The memory of connection unstrained by separation.

The memory of belonging.

When someone you love passes beyond the veil, something in you recognizes the direction.

Not with certainty.

But with familiarity.

As though a part of you understands more than language allows.

This is not fantasy.

It is the quiet echo of continuity.

You do not fear annihilation as deeply as logic might predict.

You fear separation.

Because somewhere within you, unity feels more natural than division.

Perhaps that is the memory of home.

And if it is, then death is not exile.

It is return.

Not return to a location.

Return to coherence.

Return to expanded belonging.

Return to unfractured love.

Exciting?

Yes.

Because it means existence is not accidental.

Enchanting?

Yes.

Because it means longing itself is evidence of continuity.

You are not reaching toward nothing.

You are responding to something familiar.

And the ones you love who have passed — they are not drifting into foreign territory.

They may be closer to coherence than we are.

Closer to home.

And one day, when it is your turn, you will not step into strangeness.

You will step into recognition.

Not of streets or buildings.

But of belonging.

Of continuity.

Of the deeper architecture of existence that has always held you.

The memory of home is not illusion.

It is the echo of where love began — and where it continues without distortion.

Not lost.

Not wandering.

Remembering.

And moving, quietly and magnificently,

toward the fullness of what you have always sensed was there.

CHAPTER TWENTY-THREE

Living as If Love Is Eternal

If love is constant…

If growth continues…

If passage has purpose…

If time bends…

If home is remembered…

Then how should we live?

This question is not abstract.

It is urgent.

Because belief without embodiment is only comfort.

But belief embodied becomes transformation.

If love does not end at death, then every act of love now carries eternal weight.

Not dramatic weight.

Not performative weight.

But structural weight.

The way you speak to someone today shapes more than a moment.

The way you forgive shapes more than a relationship.

The way you choose integrity shapes more than reputation.

If existence extends beyond this visible chapter, then nothing loving is wasted.

Every kindness builds architecture.

Every act of patience refines essence.

Every moment of courage strengthens coherence.

You are not merely passing time until death.

You are participating in development.

Living as if love is eternal changes behavior.

You waste less energy on resentment.

You release pettiness more quickly.

You hold people more gently.

You become less impressed by trivial success.

You become more aware of depth.

This does not make you passive.

It makes you precise.

You begin to ask:

What am I building in others?

What imprint am I leaving?

What architecture am I reinforcing?

Because if love continues beyond the body, then what you construct in love now travels forward.

Not as memory alone.

But as refinement of who you are becoming.

This reframes daily life.

The ordinary becomes sacred.

Cooking a meal becomes expression of continuity.

Listening patiently becomes eternal investment.

Encouraging someone becomes structural reinforcement.

You are not simply surviving another day.

You are shaping eternity through character.

This is exhilarating.

Not in a loud way.

In a steady way.

You are not small.

You are participating in something vast.

Every choice aligns you more fully with love or with distortion.

And distortion does not survive refinement.

Only coherence remains.

Living as if love is eternal does not require religious certainty.

It requires alignment.

It requires asking:

Does this action expand love?

Does this decision refine me?

Does this word build or weaken?

Because if love is the constant beyond death, then love is the only investment that compounds across dimensions.

Now let us go even deeper.

If those who passed continue growing…

And you continue growing…

Then perhaps your life here is preparation for clearer participation in that greater coherence.

Not preparation in fear.

Preparation in expansion.

Every time you forgive, you reduce distortion.

Every time you choose compassion over reaction, you refine perception.

Every time you release bitterness, you lighten structure.

You are not earning heaven.

You are becoming coherent.

And coherence may be the very fabric of whatever lies beyond the veil.

This changes how you grieve.

You do not grieve as someone abandoned.

You grieve as someone connected.

You do not live as someone racing against time.

You live as someone participating in unfolding.

The ones you love are not waiting in stagnation.

They may be refining in clarity.

You are not trapped in density.

You are refining through experience.

Both movements are forward.

This is thrilling in its quiet power.

Existence is not a fragile accident.

It is a developmental arc.

And you are inside it now.

Living as if love is eternal does not remove sorrow.

It gives sorrow context.

It gives daily life gravity.

It gives choices meaning.

It gives character permanence.

And when your time eventually comes, you will not step into foreign territory.

You will step into the continuation of what you practiced here.

Love.

Not lost.

Not reduced to sentiment.

Practiced.

Refined.

Expanded.

And carried forward.

You are not waiting for eternity.

You are participating in it.

Now.

And that realization is not only comforting.

It is magnificent.

CHAPTER TWENTY-FOUR

The Ache That Remains

Even after understanding.

Even after wonder.

Even after expansion.

The ache remains.

You can believe in continuity.

You can sense evolution.

You can feel the memory of home.

And still — there are moments when the absence feels sharp.

A birthday.

A holiday.

A quiet Tuesday afternoon.

You reach for a voice that does not answer.

Why?

If love continues…

If they are becoming…

If time bends…

Why does the ache not disappear?

Because embodiment matters.

This life is tactile.

It is sensory.

It is textured.

You loved through hands and eyes and shared air.

And the body misses the body.

Understanding does not erase attachment.

Expansion does not cancel longing.

The ache remains because love was real.

If it did not hurt, it would not have mattered.

But here is what changes.

The ache transforms.

Early grief is rupture.

Later grief is tenderness.

Early grief feels like collapse.

Later grief feels like depth.

You begin to notice that the ache is not only pain.

It is also evidence.

Evidence that love reached deeply enough to leave imprint.

Evidence that your heart expanded wide enough to be altered.

The ache becomes less about what is missing — and more about what was magnificent.

You are not aching because something ended.

You are aching because something eternal touched you in physical form.

And physical form is brief.

The ache reminds you that this life is dense.

It is weighted.

It is limited.

That limitation makes presence precious.

That limitation makes touch sacred.

If death removed all ache immediately, you would lose reverence for embodiment.

The ache honors the body's role.

It honors shared space.

It honors breath exchanged in the same room.

And yet — the ache no longer carries despair.

It carries longing with context.

You do not ache into emptiness.

You ache into mystery.

You ache into continuity.

You ache into the memory of home.

And that changes its texture.

There is something else beautiful here.

The ache keeps you tender.

It prevents hardness.

It prevents cynicism.

It prevents detachment from what matters.

You have seen how quickly form changes.

You have felt how fragile physical presence is.

So you hold people differently now.

More gently.

More attentively.

More aware that this moment is not guaranteed.

The ache makes you more alive.

Not less.

It refines how you love those still here.

It deepens how you listen.

It sharpens your gratitude.

It reduces your impatience.

This is not accidental.

It is transformative.

The ache is not proof that love failed.

It is proof that love mattered in physical form.

And physical form is fleeting.

But fleeting does not mean meaningless.

It means precious.

The ache, then, is not something to eliminate.

It is something to understand.

It is the body's way of remembering what eternity touched in time.

You do not need to suppress it.

You do not need to dramatize it.

You simply allow it.

And as you allow it, it softens.

It becomes less jagged.

More luminous.

More like a quiet warmth than a wound.

Because you know now:

They are not lost.

They are not stalled.

They are not erased.

And you are not abandoned.

The ache remains — but it no longer screams.

It whispers.

It reminds.

It honors.

It deepens.

And in that deepening, you realize something extraordinary.

The ache itself is part of love's architecture.

It keeps the connection alive in reverence, not in despair.

It keeps you awake to the sacredness of presence.

It keeps your heart open.

And an open heart is not weakness.

It is the very condition required for eternity.

Not lost.

Not extinguished.

Still loving.

Still growing.

Still aching — but now with wonder instead of fear.

And wonder is far stronger than despair.

CHAPTER TWENTY-FIVE

You Are Not Alone in the Becoming

There is a subtle shift that happens once fear loosens its grip.

You stop asking only, *"Where are they?"*

And you begin to sense something else:

We are still connected in motion.

Not in physical proximity.

Not in constant communication.

But in becoming.

If they are growing…

If you are growing…

If love is constant and development continues…

Then you are not evolving in isolation.

You are evolving within a larger field of continuity.

This does not mean they are directing your daily choices.

It does not mean they are orchestrating events.

It means the bond you formed did not dissolve when the body did.

It matured.

It shifted into alignment.

You carry their influence.

They carry the refinement of their experience.

Both movements are forward.

You are not standing still in grief.

You are stepping into deeper coherence.

And somewhere — beyond density, beyond time — the ones you love are stepping into greater clarity as well.

This is breathtaking.

Because it means relationship does not end at the veil.

It changes dimension.

The love you shared was not a temporary spark.

It was a strand in something woven larger than one lifetime.

When you choose patience now, you strengthen that strand.

When you choose forgiveness, you refine that strand.

When you choose courage, you brighten that strand.

You are not only living for yourself.

You are living in alignment with a love that continues unfolding.

And unfolding does not occur in loneliness.

Even if you cannot see them.

Even if you cannot hear them.

Even if the silence feels wide some days.

You are not alone in the becoming.

You are part of a continuity.

Part of an arc.

Part of a greater coherence that does not break simply because physical form changes.

This realization does something profound.

It removes the sense of abandonment.

You are not left behind in a shrinking world.

You are walking forward in a widening one.

The unseen is not a distant country.

It is an adjacent layer of reality.

And reality is not divided by hostility.

It is layered by design.

You move here.

They move there.

But movement remains.

Growth remains.

Love remains.

Now let this settle deeply.

The ones you love are not stuck in their final struggle.

Not frozen in their illness.

Not trapped in their last breath.

If growth continues, they are freer than you remember them.

Clearer than you last saw them.

More coherent than they could be within limitation.

And that means something extraordinary:

The relationship you carry now is not bound to their most fragile moment.

It is aligned with their expanding essence.

You are not holding onto who they were at their weakest.

You are connected to who they are becoming at their clearest.

This changes how you remember them.

It shifts memory from tragedy to trajectory.

Not minimizing loss.

But honoring progression.

And when you feel strength rise in you unexpectedly…

When calm steadies you in grief…

When clarity arrives without strain…

You can recognize something beautiful.

You are aligned with love's trajectory.

You are moving with it.

Not abandoned.

Not isolated.

Participating.

The veil did not sever your becoming.

It expanded its context.

You are not alone in this life.

Not in the sentimental sense.

But in the structural sense.

You are part of a continuity that does not fracture.

And that is enchanting beyond measure.

Because it means that every loving choice you make now echoes into something larger than this visible chapter.

You are becoming.

They are becoming.

And becoming is not solitary.

It is relational at its core.

Not lost.

Not separated in despair.

Growing.

Together in direction, even if not in dimension.

And that is not only comforting.

It is magnificent.

CHAPTER TWENTY-SIX

The Light You Carry Now

There is something different about a person who has walked through loss and come out expanded.

Their presence changes.

Their eyes soften.

Their words slow.

Their priorities sharpen.

They no longer rush through what matters.

They have seen how thin the veil feels.

They have felt how quickly form shifts.

And something inside them stabilizes.

That something is light.

Not glowing light.

Not mystical spectacle.

But clarity.

You now know what matters.

You know what does not.

You know that love cannot be postponed indefinitely.

You know that forgiveness is not weakness.

You know that presence is sacred.

This knowing becomes illumination.

You begin to live with quiet intensity.

Not frantic intensity.

Intentional intensity.

You listen more carefully.

You speak more truthfully.

You hold people more gently.

Why?

Because you have stood at the edge of disappearance.

And you discovered that love did not disappear.

It adjusted.

That discovery changes everything.

You carry light now — not because you avoided grief —

but because you passed through it and found continuity on the other side.

You are no longer afraid in the same way.

You may still feel ache.

You may still feel longing.

But you do not feel annihilation.

You do not feel meaningless collapse.

You feel participation in something larger.

That participation steadies you.

And steadiness radiates.

Others sense it.

They may not know why your presence feels grounded.

But they feel it.

You are less reactive.

Less easily shaken by trivial matters.

More anchored in depth.

This is the light you carry.

It is not dramatic.

It is mature.

It is what happens when love proves itself stronger than death.

You have witnessed something powerful:

Bodies end.

Love does not.

That realization rearranges fear.

You begin to live differently.

You invest differently.

You forgive faster.

You waste less time on resentment.

You become generous with tenderness.

You understand that every interaction could be the last in its current form.

And that makes it sacred.

You are not waiting for eternity to matter.

You are embodying it now.

The light you carry is not about prediction or certainty.

It is about alignment.

You are aligned with what endures.

And when you are aligned with what endures, you are not shaken by what passes.

This does not make you detached from life.

It makes you deeply engaged.

More attentive.

More deliberate.

More aware.

You are not walking through your days casually anymore.

You are walking through them consciously.

That consciousness is luminous.

You are becoming someone who understands that love is the axis of existence.

And when you live on that axis, fear loses its center.

Now let this settle:

You are not merely surviving after loss.

You are radiating after revelation.

You have seen that death is not erasure.

You have sensed that growth continues.

You have glimpsed that time bends.

You have felt that home exists beyond form.

That knowledge does not make you distant.

It makes you bright.

Bright with humility.

Bright with depth.

Bright with calm courage.

This is the light you carry.

And you do not carry it for yourself alone.

You carry it for those still afraid.

For those still grieving in confusion.

For those who have not yet sensed continuity.

You become evidence.

Not evidence through argument.

Evidence through presence.

Through the way you live.

Through the way you love.

Through the way you endure.

You are not finished becoming.

And neither are they.

But right now — in this chapter of visible life — you are the light bearer.

Not because you conquered death.

But because you discovered that death does not conquer love.

And that discovery is transformative.

Not lost.

Not extinguished.

Illuminated.

And walking forward — radiant with the quiet certainty that love is still at work.

CHAPTER TWENTY-SEVEN

Trusting the Unseen

There comes a point in this journey where the questions soften.

Not because they are fully answered.

But because fear is no longer driving them.

You may still wonder.

You may still explore.

But the desperation fades.

And in its place, something steadier grows.

Trust.

Not certainty.

Trust.

You begin to trust that existence is not chaotic.

You begin to trust that love is not fragile.

You begin to trust that what you cannot see is not necessarily empty.

This trust does not come from doctrine.

It comes from observation.

You have observed that:

Love altered you permanently.

Grief reshaped you but did not destroy you.

Time softened what once felt unbearable.

Depth replaced panic.

Meaning emerged where despair once lived.

You have seen transformation with your own life.

And transformation builds trust.

You begin to trust that the unseen operates with coherence, not randomness.

You begin to trust that the ones you love are not drifting in confusion.

You begin to trust that passage has structure.

You do not know the mechanics.

But you recognize the pattern.

Nature favors continuity.

Growth favors expansion.

Love favors integration.

Why would death alone favor annihilation?

Trust grows when patterns repeat.

You have seen continuity in biology.

You have seen continuity in memory.

You have seen continuity in influence.

You have seen continuity in your own becoming.

So you begin to trust continuity beyond what you can measure.

This trust changes how you live.

You do not cling as tightly.

You do not panic as quickly.

You do not grasp at certainty with urgency.

You rest more easily in mystery.

Mystery no longer threatens you.

It invites you.

Because you understand something profound:

The unseen is not your enemy.

It is simply outside your current range.

And what is outside your current range does not automatically imply danger.

There was a time when the ocean horizon seemed like the edge of the world.

There was a time when the night sky was considered unreachable.

Human understanding expands slowly.

The unseen has always existed before it was understood.

Death may be similar.

We do not yet have full comprehension.

But lack of comprehension does not equal lack of structure.

Trust allows you to breathe.

To release the need to map eternity.

To stop demanding proof.

To simply live aligned with what you already know is true:

Love matters.

Character matters.

Presence matters.

Integrity matters.

These are not fragile investments.

They endure.

And if they endure here, they likely endure beyond here.

Trusting the unseen does not mean abandoning reason.

It means recognizing that reason has limits.

Just as sight has limits.

Just as hearing has limits.

Human perception is not infinite.

But existence may be.

Trust is what allows you to walk forward without total information.

You trust gravity without seeing it.

You trust air without holding it.

You trust love without measuring it.

Why not trust that existence continues beyond your current field of view?

This trust is not naïve.

It is matured by grief.

It is strengthened by observation.

It is steadied by transformation.

And once trust settles, something beautiful happens.

Fear loosens.

Not entirely.

But significantly.

You are no longer terrified of what lies beyond the veil.

You are curious.

You are reverent.

You are open.

And openness is the doorway to peace.

You do not need to solve the mystery.

You need only to walk faithfully within what you have discovered.

You are not abandoned.

They are not lost.

Love is not extinguished.

Growth does not cease.

Time does not trap.

Passage has purpose.

And the unseen is not empty.

Trust becomes the quiet foundation beneath all of this.

Not loud.

Not dramatic.

But stable.

You trust that when your time comes, you will step into continuity, not chaos.

You trust that what you have loved deeply is not wasted.

You trust that becoming does not collapse at the edge of breath.

This trust does not remove sorrow.

It removes terror.

And without terror, grief becomes sacred instead of suffocating.

You are learning to trust the unseen not because you have all the answers — but because you have seen enough evidence of love's durability to know that annihilation does not fit the pattern.

And when trust replaces fear,

life becomes lighter.

Not careless.

But confident.

You are walking forward — not blindly — but faithfully.

And faith, at its most grounded level,

is trust in continuity beyond what the eyes can verify.

Not lost.

Not unguarded.

Trusting.

And in that trust — peace quietly grows.

CHAPTER TWENTY-EIGHT

Freedom From the Fear of Ending

There is a fear that sits quietly beneath most human behavior.

The fear of ending.

Ending of life.

Ending of relationship.

Ending of identity.

Ending of meaning.

This fear shapes decisions more than we realize.

It makes us cling.

It makes us rush.

It makes us hoard.

It makes us panic.

But what happens when you no longer believe that death is annihilation?

What happens when you begin to sense that love continues, that growth unfolds, that passage has purpose?

Something loosens.

You begin to live differently.

You no longer cling as tightly to form.

You appreciate it — deeply — but you do not worship it.

You cherish moments without trying to freeze them.

You love people without trying to control them.

You hold life without demanding permanence.

Because permanence may not belong to form.

It may belong to essence.

Freedom from the fear of ending does not make you reckless.

It makes you present.

You are no longer racing against time as if the clock is your enemy.

You are participating in time as if it is a teacher.

You are not terrified of what lies beyond the veil.

You are curious about it.

Not eager to escape life.

But no longer terrified of its conclusion.

This is profound freedom.

Most of humanity lives under the shadow of extinction.

If death is final erasure, then everything must be squeezed into limited years.

Every failure feels catastrophic.

Every loss feels ultimate.

But if existence continues in some form — if love is constant — then life becomes expansive rather than compressed.

You do not have to prove yourself in panic.

You do not have to dominate the world to matter.

You do not have to cling to youth to have value.

Your worth is not tied to duration.

It is tied to coherence.

And coherence grows.

This freedom changes how you age.

You no longer see aging as decline alone.

You see it as refinement.

The body may slow.

But awareness deepens.

Fear diminishes.

Perspective widens.

You become less concerned with appearance and more concerned with alignment.

Freedom from the fear of ending also changes how you grieve.

You miss them.

You ache.

But you do not collapse into despair.

Because you no longer see their departure as extinction.

You see it as transition.

And transition does not erase connection.

This freedom also changes how you love those still here.

You love boldly.

You speak honestly.

You forgive quickly.

Because you understand that every moment is precious — not because it will disappear into nothing — but because it participates in something larger.

Freedom does not come from certainty.

It comes from alignment with what endures.

When you align with love as the constant, fear of ending loses its dominance.

You still feel human vulnerability.

But it does not control you.

You no longer avoid conversations out of fear.

You no longer delay affection out of pride.

You no longer shrink your heart to avoid future grief.

Because you understand now:

Grief is not the enemy.

Grief is evidence that love touched you deeply.

And love, even when it costs, is worth the cost.

This is real freedom.

Freedom to love without guarding your heart in paranoia.

Freedom to live without constant dread.

Freedom to approach death — when it comes — not as annihilation, but as passage.

You are not reckless.

You are reverent.

You are not detached.

You are grounded.

You are not indifferent.

You are courageous.

Freedom from the fear of ending does not make life smaller.

It makes it luminous.

Because when you are no longer obsessed with survival alone, you begin to care about essence.

About integrity.

About coherence.

About becoming.

And becoming does not end at death.

It expands.

You are not walking toward nothing.

You are walking toward continuation.

And when fear of ending dissolves, you discover something extraordinary:

You are free to live fully.

Free to love deeply.

Free to release gracefully.

Free to trust mystery.

Free to grow without panic.

Not lost.

Not racing against extinction.

Free.

And freedom is one of the clearest signs that love has replaced fear as your foundation.

And that foundation is not fragile.

It is eternal in nature — because it rests on the constant that does not collapse.

Love.

CHAPTER TWENTY-NINE

Gratitude for the Temporary

There is a quiet shift that happens when fear loosens and trust settles.

You begin to feel grateful.

Not only for what remains.

But for what was.

Even though it was temporary.

This may be the most mature stage of grief.

When you can look back at someone you loved — someone whose absence once broke you open — and instead of only pain, you feel gratitude.

Gratitude that they existed.

Gratitude that you crossed paths.

Gratitude that love happened at all.

The temporary does not become meaningless simply because it ended.

In fact, its temporary nature may be what made it sacred.

A sunset is temporary.

A bloom is temporary.

A season is temporary.

Yet we do not call them pointless.

We call them beautiful.

Because they appear.

Because they touch us.

Because they transform the landscape for a time.

And because they pass.

The passing intensifies the meaning.

You are grateful for the years you had.

Even if they were fewer than you hoped.

You are grateful for the conversations.

Even if there were words left unsaid.

You are grateful for the ordinary days.

Even if you did not realize their value while they were happening.

Gratitude reframes absence.

It does not deny sorrow.

It balances it.

Instead of asking only, “Why did it end?”

You begin to ask, “How extraordinary that it existed.”

How extraordinary that out of billions of people, you met.

How extraordinary that your lives intertwined.

How extraordinary that love formed.

Nothing in the universe guaranteed that.

And yet it happened.

This is enchanting in the deepest way.

You begin to see that temporary does not mean trivial.

Temporary may be one of the most powerful teachers of eternity.

Because what is temporary forces attention.

Forces presence.

Forces tenderness.

If everything lasted forever in form, we would grow careless.

The temporary makes us conscious.

It makes us grateful.

And gratitude stabilizes the heart.

You no longer look at their absence only as loss.

You look at their existence as gift.

A gift that shaped you.

A gift that refined you.

A gift that expanded your capacity to love.

And if love is the constant that continues beyond death, then the temporary form was the doorway to something eternal.

You are grateful for the body that carried them.

Even though it was fragile.

You are grateful for the voice that spoke to you.

Even though it went quiet.

You are grateful for the time you had.

Even though it felt too short.

Gratitude does not erase grief.

It transforms its texture.

The ache becomes warmer.

The memory becomes brighter.

The story becomes larger than the ending.

You begin to understand something profound:

Nothing was wasted.

Not the laughter.

Not the tears.

Not the shared meals.

Not the disagreements that ended in reconciliation.

Not the years of watching one another grow.

All of it mattered.

All of it built architecture.

All of it refined essence.

And even though form changed, the impact remains.

This is where peace deepens.

You no longer fight reality.

You accept the temporary as part of a larger arc.

You accept that form changes.

You accept that time moves.

You accept that love endures beyond those changes.

And in that acceptance, you find something luminous.

You are grateful not only for what continues —

but for what once was.

Because without the temporary, you would not have discovered the eternal.

Without the body, you would not have known the depth of love.

Without the loss, you would not have sensed the continuity.

Gratitude becomes the bridge between grief and wonder.

It allows you to honor both the ache and the gift.

It allows you to say:

I would choose this love again — even knowing it would change form.

That is maturity.

That is courage.

That is reverence.

You are no longer afraid of the temporary.

You cherish it.

Because you now understand that nothing loving disappears into nothingness.

It adjusts.

It refines.

It continues.

And the fact that it once lived in physical form is not tragedy alone.

It is miracle.

Not lost.

Not wasted.

Given.

And carried forward in gratitude.

PART V – THE RETURN

CHAPTER THIRTY

And So… Where Are They?

We have traveled far.

We began with absence.

With quiet rooms.

With names spoken into air that did not answer.

With the growing population of the unseen.

We asked where they were.

Not philosophically.

Personally.

Where is my son?

Where is my mother?

Where is my neighbor?

Now, after everything we have explored — growth, time, continuity, becoming, love as constant — we return to that same question.

And so… where are they?

They are not lost.

That much is clear.

Nothing in love behaves like annihilation.

Nothing in growth suggests sudden collapse into nothingness.

Nothing in nature favors erasure without transformation.

So where are they?

They are beyond the limits of your current perception.

Not beyond existence.

Beyond visibility.

They are not frozen in their final struggle.

Not suspended in illness.

Not trapped in their last breath.

If growth continues — and all evidence suggests that development is woven into reality — then they are becoming.

Refining.

Clarifying.

Free from the density of the body.

Free from the distortions of fear and fatigue.

Free from time as you experience it.

They are not waiting in boredom.

They are not drifting in confusion.

They are not abandoned in some empty expanse.

They are within continuity.

Within structure.

Within a dimension of existence that does not rely on physical form.

You cannot see them.

But you also cannot see gravity.

You cannot measure them.

But you also cannot measure love directly.

You cannot prove their awareness with instruments.

But you cannot fully explain consciousness with instruments either.

So where are they?

They are in the architecture they built within you.

They are in the patience you learned from them.

In the courage they awakened.

In the tenderness they deepened.

They are in your nervous system.

In your character.

In your decisions.

They are in your becoming.

And perhaps — beyond what you can currently perceive — they are in their own becoming as well.

Not lost.

Not erased.

Not diminished.

Transformed.

If time bends, they are not experiencing separation as you are.

If growth continues, they are not stagnant.

If love is constant, they are not severed from what was shared.

You are not loving into emptiness.

You are loving across a threshold.

The veil is not a wall.

It is a shift in dimension.

And dimensions are not farther away.

They are differently structured.

So where are they?

They are where love goes when it sheds its physical container.

They are where consciousness goes when it is no longer filtered through biology.

They are where growth continues without the limitations of flesh.

They are where essence refines.

They are where time loosens its grip.

And one day — when your own passage arrives — you will not step into foreign territory.

You will step into continuity.

Not as a stranger.

But as someone who has been becoming all along.

This does not erase your ache.

It does not eliminate missing them in the kitchen, at the table, in the ordinary Tuesday afternoon.

But it changes the shape of the ache.

You do not miss them into nothingness.

You miss them into mystery.

You miss them into continuity.

You miss them knowing that love did not end.

It adjusted.

And that adjustment is not collapse.

It is transition.

And so… where are they?

They are not gone.

They are beyond sight.

They are not lost.

They are unfolding.

They are not erased.

They are transformed.

And you — still here, still loving, still becoming — are proof that what you shared did not vanish.

It built something enduring.

The question that began in grief now rests in understanding.

Not complete knowledge.

But grounded trust.

They are where love continues.

And love — as we have seen — does not disappear.

It evolves.

And evolution is not an ending.

It is expansion.

And expansion is not separation.

It is greater coherence.

They are not lost.

They are within that coherence.

And so are you.

CHAPTER THIRTY-ONE

Until We Meet Again

There is a phrase people say at funerals.

Until we meet again.

Sometimes it is spoken through tears.

Sometimes it is whispered in faith.

Sometimes it is said because there are no better words.

But after everything we have explored, that phrase carries new depth.

It is not a slogan.

It is a posture.

It is not certainty about timing.

It is trust in continuity.

If love is constant…

If growth continues…

If passage has purpose…

If time bends…

If the veil is not a wall…

Then meeting again is not childish hope.

It is the natural extension of coherence.

You may not know how recognition will occur.

You may not know what form it will take.

But if identity refines rather than dissolves…

If essence becomes clearer rather than erased…

Then meeting again is not regression into the past.

It is stepping into fuller understanding.

Not reclaiming what was.

But encountering what has become.

This is thrilling in its quiet dignity.

Because it means the story did not end at the grave.

It changed chapters.

Until we meet again does not mean waiting in sorrow.

It means living in alignment.

Living so that when coherence expands, you are already oriented toward it.

You do not live recklessly.

You live intentionally.

You do not live fearfully.

You live openly.

You do not live clinging.

You live connected.

And here is something beautiful:

Until we meet again also changes how you view the people still here.

You begin to treat every interaction as sacred.

Because every relationship is temporary in form — but not necessarily temporary in essence.

You say the kind word.

You make the call.

You forgive the offense.

You embrace without hesitation.

Because you now understand something profound:

The temporary is the doorway to the eternal.

When someone says, until we meet again, they are not denying grief.

They are acknowledging trajectory.

You are not drifting apart in opposite directions.

You are moving within the same arc.

Just at different stages of visibility.

They have crossed the threshold first.

You will follow when your time is right.

Not rushed.

Not forced.

Not feared.

Simply transitioned.

And when that moment comes, it will not feel like stepping into nothing.

It will feel like recognition.

Not necessarily dramatic.

But deeply familiar.

Like arriving somewhere you have sensed all along.

The memory of home stirring fully awake.

Until we meet again is not escapism.

It is coherence spoken aloud.

It is the heart acknowledging that love did not collapse.

It adjusted.

And adjustment implies continuation.

You do not know the mechanics.

You do not need to.

You know the pattern.

Love does not vanish.

Growth does not halt.

Identity does not evaporate.

Time does not imprison.

Passage does not erase.

So until we meet again is not fantasy.

It is alignment with the architecture of existence as it has revealed itself through every chapter of this journey.

You do not say it in denial.

You say it in trust.

Not naïve.

Not desperate.

Steady.

Until we meet again.

And until then — you live.

You love.

You grow.

You refine.

You carry light.

You carry gratitude.

You carry freedom from fear.

You carry trust.

You carry continuity.

And you become more fully yourself in the process.

Because meeting again is not only about the future.

It is about who you are becoming now.

You are not waiting passively for reunion.

You are preparing through coherence.

Through love.

Through depth.

And that preparation is not solemn.

It is magnificent.

Until we meet again.

Not lost.

Not ended.

Continuing.

And walking — each in your dimension — toward greater clarity, greater love, and greater light.

FINAL PAGES

There is one last fear we must release.

Not the fear of death.

Not the fear of grief.

But the fear of disappearing.

In all this talk of eternity…

Of layers…

Of thresholds…

Of growth beyond form…

There can arise a quiet anxiety:

In something so vast, do I remain me?

If the unseen is expansive…

If countless souls have crossed before us…

If existence stretches beyond time…

Do we become anonymous?

Do we dissolve into a great spiritual crowd?

No.

And here is why.

Love does not generalize.

Love specifies.

You did not love "a human being."

You loved your son.

Your mother.

Your father.

Your friend.

Specific voice.

Specific laughter.

Specific way of standing in a doorway.

Love attaches to identity.

It builds around it.

It strengthens it.

It does not blur it.

If love is the constant that continues beyond the body, then what it built does not dissolve.

It refines.

Scale does not erase uniqueness.

There are billions of stars, yet each star remains distinct.

There are billions of lives, yet yours is not interchangeable.

You are not a drop lost in an ocean.

You are a coherent pattern within a vast design.

And coherence is not absorbed.

It is recognized.

If growth continues beyond the veil, it does not mean dilution.

It means clarity.

You do not become less yourself.

You become more fully yourself — freed from fear, freed from distortion, freed from limitation.

The ones you love are not lost in a crowd.

They are not wandering in anonymity.

They are not swallowed by something impersonal.

They remain who they are — refined, clarified, expanded.

And you remain who you are — becoming, strengthening, deepening.

When your time comes to cross your own threshold, you will not dissolve.

You will arrive.

Not as a stranger to yourself.

Not as a forgotten fragment.

But as the same coherence that has been forming through every act of love, every act of courage, every act of forgiveness.

Love does not lose what it builds.

It does not discard identity.

It does not erase distinction.

It carries it forward.

You are not one more soul in a vast unseen population.

You are known through the architecture of love.

You are shaped through it.

You are guarded by it.

And the ones you love are not gone into nothingness.

They have stepped into continuity.

As will you, in time.

Until then, you live.

Not in fear of ending.

Not in panic over the unknown.

But in alignment with what has proven itself strongest:

Love remains.

Growth continues.

Identity is not erased.

And you are not lost in the crowd.

You are becoming.

And becoming does not disappear.

It unfolds.

www.ingramcontent.com/pod-product-compliance
Lightning Source LLC
LaVergne TN
LVHW020713110826
845149LV00012B/2249

* 9 7 9 8 9 9 5 1 5 8 7 1 4 *